How To Reduce Landlord Taxes

Tax Saving Tips To Help Boost Your Property Profits!

By

Arthur Weller, Sarah Bradford & Amer Siddiq

Publisher Details
This guide is published by Tax Portal Ltd. 3 Sanderson Close, Great Sankey, Warrington, Cheshire, WA5 3LN.

'How to Reduce Landlord Taxes' – First published in May 2009. Second Edition April 2010. Third Edition July 2010. Fourth Edition April 2011. Fifth Edition April 2012. Sixth Edition April 2013. Seventh edition May 2014. Eighth edition April 2015. Ninth Edition April 2016. Tenth Edition April 2017. Eleventh Edition April 2018. Twelfth Edition March 2019. Thirteenth Edition May 2020. Fourteenth Edition April 2021.Fifteenth Edition April 2022.Sixteenth Edition April 2023. Seventeenth Edition April 2024.

Copyright
The right of Sarah Bradford, Arthur Weller and Tax Portal Ltd to be identified as the authors of this guide has been asserted in accordance with the Copyright, Designs and Patents Act 1988, England.

© 2009-2025 Arthur Weller, Sarah Bradford and Tax Portal Ltd

A CIP Copy of this book is available from the British Library.

978-1-7394153-4-1

All rights reserved
All rights reserved. No part of this guide may be reproduced or transmitted in any form or by any means, electronically or mechanically, including photocopying, recording or any information storage or retrieval system, without prior permission in writing from the publisher.

Permission is granted to print a single hardcopy version of this guide for your personal use only.

Trademarks
Property Tax Portal, Tax Portal Ltd and other Tax Portal Ltd services/ products referenced in this guide are registered trademarks or trademarks of Tax Portal Ltd in the UK and/or other countries.

Disclaimer

1. This guide is produced for General guidance only, and professional advice should be sought before any decision is made. Individual circumstances can vary and therefore no responsibility can be accepted by the authors or the publisher Tax Portal Ltd, for any action taken, or any decision made to refrain from action, by any readers of this guide.

2. Tax rules and legislation are constantly changing and therefore the information printed in this guide is correct at the time of printing – April 2024.

3. Neither the authors nor Tax Portal Ltd offer financial, legal or investment advice. If you require such advice then, we urge you to seek the opinion of an appropriate professional in the relevant field. We care about your success and therefore encourage you to take appropriate advice before you put any of your financial or other resources at risk. Don't forget, investment values can decrease as well as increase.

4. To the fullest extent permitted by law, the authors and Tax Portal Ltd do not accept liability for any direct, indirect, special, consequential or other losses or damages of whatsoever kind arising from using this guide.

    The guide itself is provided 'as is' without express or implied warranty.

5. The authors and Tax Portal Ltd reserve the right to alter any part of this guide at any time without notice.

Contents

1. About The Authors 13

    1.1. **Sarah Bradford – Tax Specialist** _____ 13

    1.2. **Arthur Weller - Tax Specialist** _____ 13

    1.3. **Amer Siddiq - The Landlord** _____ 14

    1.4. **Acknowledgements** _____ 14

2. The Importance Of Tax Planning 15

    2.1. **Knowing When To Consider Planning** _____ 15

        2.1.1. Buying 15
        2.1.2. Repairs And Refurbishment 16
        2.1.3. Selling 16
        2.1.4. Life Changes 17
        2.1.5. Politics 17
        2.1.6. End And Start Of The Tax Year 17

    2.2. **The Real Benefits Of Tax Planning** _____ 18

        2.2.1. Paying Less Tax 18
        2.2.2. Clear 'Entrance' And 'Exit' Strategies 18
        2.2.3. Staying Focused 18
        2.2.4. Improving Cash Flow 19
        2.2.5. Avoiding Common Tax Traps 19

    2.3. **Asking HMRC For Tax Advice** _____ 19

        2.3.1. Making Use Of HMRC Services 19
        2.3.2. The Drawback 20
        2.3.3. Practical Tip 20

3. Making Tax Digital For Landlords 21

    3.1. **What Is Making Tax Digital?** _____ 21

    3.2. **What Will Stay The Same?** _____ 21

    3.3. **Submission Dates** _____ 22

        3.3.1. Number Of Submissions 22
        3.3.2. 'Real Time Basis' 22

    3.4. **When Is MTD Starting?** _____ 23

        3.4.1. Stage 1 23
        3.4.2. Stages 2 And 3 23
        3.4.3. Which Landlords Will Be Affected? 23

    3.5. **MTD Compliance** _____ 23

        3.5.1. All Landlords 23
        3.5.2. Practical Tip 24

		3.5.3.	Multiple Properties..24
		3.5.4.	Jointly Owned Properties..24
		3.5.5.	How And When Will Tax Payments Be Made?..24

    3.6.   The New System Of Penalties   **24**

		3.6.1.	Late Submission...24
		3.6.2.	Late Payment Regime..25
		3.6.3.	First Year..25

    3.7.   Simplified 'Cash Basis' For Unincorporated Property Businesses   **25**

    3.8.   Possible Timetable For 2026/27 And 2027/8   **25**

    3.9.   Final Points   **26**

    3.10.   Invest In Landlord Software   **26**

4. *Understanding Your Tax Liabilities* 27

5. *Income Tax Liabilities For Investors/Traders* 30

    5.1.   Property Investor   **30**

    5.2.   Property Traders/Dealers   **30**

    5.3.   Income Tax Rates   **30**

    5.4.   Income Tax Calculation Case Studies   **31**

		5.4.1.	Income Tax Calculation For Property Investors..31
		5.4.2.	Income Tax Calculation For Property Developers.....................................33

6. *Owning Properties As A Sole Trader* 35

    6.1.   Buying Properties As A Sole Trader   **35**

    6.2.   When Is It Tax Efficient To Buy Property As A Sole Trader?   **35**

    6.3.   When Is It NOT Tax Efficient To Buy Property As A Sole Trader?   **36**

    6.4.   A Note About Selling Properties When Operating As A Sole Trader   **36**

7. *Legal v Beneficial Ownership: A 'Taxing' Distinction!* 37

    7.1.   Legal And Beneficial Ownership   **37**

    7.2.   Legal Ownership   **37**

    7.3.   Beneficial Ownership   **37**

    7.4.   Analogies   **38**

    7.5.   Tax Implications   **38**

    7.6.   Tax Complications   **39**

		7.6.1.	Income Tax..39
		7.6.2.	Capital Gains Tax..39
		7.6.3.	Inheritance Tax 39

7.6.4. Practical Tip 39

8. Offsetting Interest Charges From 6ᵗʰ April 2017 40

8.1. The New Rules _____ 40

8.2. The Restrictions _____ 40

8.3. Relevant Residential Property Lets _____ 40

8.4. What A Property Business May Consist Of _____ 40

8.5. Calculation of the restriction _____ 41

8.6. Calculation Of The Basic Rate Reducer _____ 41

9. Offsetting Different Types Of Interest Charges 42

9.1. Interest On Mortgages _____ 42

9.2. A Note About 'Interest Only' And 'Repayment Mortgages' _____ 42

9.2.1. Interest Only Mortgage 42
9.2.2. Repayment Mortgage 43

9.3. Interest On Personal Loans _____ 43

9.3.1. Loan Used For Providing Deposit 44
9.3.2. Loan Used For Refurbishments/Developments 44
9.3.3. Loans Used For Purchasing Products 45
9.3.4. Loans To Continue The Running Of Your Business 46
9.3.5. Interest On Overdrafts 46

9.4. Interest On Re-Mortgages _____ 47

10. 'Wholly And Exclusively' 50

10.1. Understanding The Term 'Wholly And Exclusively' _____ 50

10.2. What If Cost Is Not Wholly And Exclusively Incurred For Property? ___ 50

10.3. Costs Of Maintenance And Repairs _____ 51

10.4. Typical Maintenance/Repair Costs _____ 52

10.5. The Big Misconception About Costs When A Property Is First Let? ___ 52

10.5.1. Allowable Expenses 52
10.5.2. The Test 52
10.5.3. A Cinema 52
10.5.4. A Ship 53
10.5.5. Is Your Property A Cinema Or A Ship? 53

10.6. Capital Improvements _____ 53

11. Replacing Your Fixtures And Fittings 55

11.1. What Are Fixtures And Fittings? _____ 55

11.2. Replacing Fixtures And Fittings _____ 55

11.2.1.	Like-For-Like Replacement	55
11.2.2.	What If It Is Not Possible To Replace With Like-For-Like?	56
11.2.3.	Like-For-Like Replacement But With Capital Improvements	56
11.2.4.	Replacement With Superior Fixture And Fittings	57

12. Other Ways To Reduce Your Income Tax Bill 58

12.1. Rents, Rates, And Insurance — 58

12.1.1.	Rents	58
12.1.2.	Rates	58
12.1.3.	Insurance	58

12.2. Can I Offset Pre-Trading Expenditure? — 59

12.3. Carrying Over Rental Losses — 59

12.4. Claiming Travel Costs — 60

12.4.1.	'Wholly And Exclusively'	60
12.4.2.	Office Based At Home	60
12.4.3.	Office Outside Of Home	61
12.4.4.	Use Of A Letting Agent	61
12.4.5.	Relevant Tax Cases	61
12.4.6.	How Much To Claim?	61
12.4.7.	Misc. Travel Costs	62
12.4.8.	Foreign Travel	62
12.4.9.	Expenses When Not Available For Letting	62

12.5. General Property Costs — 62

12.6. Storage Costs — 63

12.7. Other Common Landlord Expenditures — 63

12.8. Can I Offset The Cost Of A Property Seminar? — 64

12.9. Capital Allowances For Landlords — 65

13. Running Your Property Business From Home 66

13.1. Nature Of Relief — 66

13.2. Typical Fixed Costs — 66

13.3. Insurance — 67

13.4. Council Tax — 67

13.5. Mortgage Costs — 67

13.6. Rent — 67

13.7. Repairs And Maintenance — 68

13.7.1.	Practical Tip	68

14. Tenant Deposits: Traps & Tips 69

14.1. Deposits From Tenants — 69

14.2.	Security Deposits	69
14.3.	Holding Deposit	70
14.3.1.	Practical Tip	71
14.4.	Tax Treatment Of 'Gifted Deposits'?	71
14.4.1.	Gifted Deposit Schemes	71
14.4.2.	Tax Treatment	72
14.4.3.	Practical Tip	72

15. *Cash Basis For Landlords* 73

15.1.	Introduction	73
15.2.	Cash Basis Vs Accruals Basis	73
15.2.1.	Nature of the Cash Basis	73
15.2.2.	Nature of the Accruals Basis	74
15.3.	Cash Basis Eligibility	74
15.4.	Election Not To Use The Cash Basis	74
15.5.	Relief For Revenue Expenses	75
15.6.	Relief For Capital Expenditure	75
15.7.	Joining Or Leaving The Cash Basis	76
15.8.	Planning Tips	76

16. *Property Partnerships and Joint Ownership* 77

16.1.	Introduction to Tax Treatment of Jointly Owned Property	77
16.2.	Is There A Partnership?	77
16.2.1.	The Legal Definition Of A Partnership	77
16.2.2.	HMRC's Approach To Determining Whether A Partnership Exists	78
16.2.3.	Case Study 1 – Letting of Jointly-Owned Property: Is There A Partnership?	79
16.3.	Formation And Dissolution Of A Partnership	80
16.3.1.	When Does The Partnership Commence?	80
16.3.2.	The Partnership Agreement	80
16.3.3.	Dissolution Of A Partnership	81
16.3.4.	Case Study 2 – Dissolution Of A Partnership – Is A New Partnership Created?	81
16.3.5.	Change Of Partners – Partnership Treated As Continuing For Tax Purposes	81
16.4.	Taxation Of Partnership Profits	81
16.4.1.	Separate Property Rental Businesses	82
16.4.2.	Case Study – Separate Property Rental Businesses	82
16.5.	Why Form A Property Partnership?	82
16.5.1.	Case Study 3 – Advantages Of A Property Partnership	83
16.6.	Joint Ownership Outside A Partnership	84

	16.6.1.	Joint Tenants And Tenants In Common	84
	16.6.2.	Joint Tenants	84
	16.6.3.	Tenants In Common	84

16.7. Joint Owners Who Are Not Spouses Or Civil Partners   85

	16.7.1.	Default Position – Profits And Losses Allocated In Ownership Shares	85
	16.7.2.	Case Study 4 – Profits Allocated In Ownership Share	85
	16.7.3.	A Different Allocation	85
		Case Study 5 – Allocation Other Than In Relation To Ownership Shares	86

16.8. Joint Owners Are Spouses And Civil Partners   86

	16.8.1.	Default Position – Profits And Losses Allocated 50:50	86
	16.8.2.	Case Study 6 – Income Allocated 50:50	87
	16.8.3.	Case Study 7 – Taking Advantage Of The 50:50 Income Allocation Rule	87
	16.8.4.	Putting A Property In Joint Names To Take Advantage Of The 50:50 Income Allocation? 88	
	16.8.5.	Case Study 8 – Putting a Proeprty In Joint Name To Take Advantage Of 50:50 Income Allocation Rule	88
	16.8.6.	Unequal Ownership Shares And A Form 17 Election	88
	16.8.7.	Case Study 9 – Benefits Of Making A Form 17 Election	89
	16.8.8.	Special Rules For Furnished Holiday Lettings	89

16.9. Other Tax Considerations   90

	16.9.1.	Capital Gains Tax	90
	16.9.2.	Case Study 10 – Making Use Of The No Gain/No Loss Rule Prior To Sale	90
	16.9.3.	SDLT, LBTT And LTT	91
	16.9.4.	Inheritance Tax	91

17. *Should Landlords Operate Through A Limited Company*   93

17.1. Pros And Cons Of Operating Through A Limited Company   93

	17.1.1.	Advantages	93
	17.1.2.	Disadvantages	95

17.2. Incorporating An Existing Property Business   96

	17.2.1.	Stamp Duty Land Tax (SDLT)	96
	17.2.2.	Capital Gains Tax (CGT)	97
	17.2.3.	Incorporation Relief	97
	17.2.4.	Disclaim Incorporation Relief Where No CGT Payable	97

17.3. Case Study 1 – Transferring Property Business To A Limited Company   98

	17.3.1.	SDLT	98
	17.3.2.	Capital Gains Tax	99
	17.3.3.	Summary	99

17.4. New Landlords – Setting Up a Property Limited Company   99

17.5. Taxation of Company Profits   99

	17.5.1.	Accruals Basis	100
	17.5.2.	Deduction For Expenses	100
	17.5.3.	Deduction For Mortgage Interest And Other Finance Costs	101

17.6. Taxation Of Capital Gains   101

17.7. Extracting Profits From The Company   102

17.7.1.	Salary	102
17.7.2.	Dividends	103
17.7.3.	Other Ways Of Extracting Funds From The Company	103
17.7.4.	Leave Profits In The Company	103

17.8. Annual Tax On Enveloped Dwellings (ATED) — 104

17.8.1.	Nature Of The ATED	104
17.8.2.	Relief For Qualifying Property Rental Businesses	104
17.8.3.	Amount Of Charge	104

17.9. Property Management Companies — 105

17.10. Property Limited Company V Unincorporated Property Business — 105

17.10.1.	Case Study 2 – Landlord Is A Basic Rate Taxpayer	106
17.10.2.	Unincorporated Property Business	106
17.10.3.	Property Company	106
17.10.4.	Comments	106

17.11. Case Study 3 – Landlord Is A Higher Rate Taxpayer — 107

17.11.1.	Unincorporated Property Business	107
17.11.2.	Property Company: Low Profits	107
17.11.3.	Case Study 5: Company Benefits from Marginal Relief	108
17.11.4.	Case Study 5: High Profits	108
17.11.5.	Final Thoughts	109

18. *Saving On Stamp Duty* 110

18.1. When Do Property Investors Pay Stamp Duty? — 110

18.1.1.	Stamp Duty When Buying New Land Or Property	110
18.1.2.	Stamp Duty When Transferring A Property	111

19. *Tax-Free Income For Renting Out Part Of Your Home* 112

19.1. What Is The Rent-A-Room Relief? — 112

19.2. Choosing Not to Use The Relief — 113

19.3. Renting Out In Joint Ownership — 114

20. *Generous Tax Breaks For Holiday Lets* 115

20.1. Qualifying Criteria For A Holiday Let — 115

20.2. Three Generous Tax Benefits Associated With Holiday Lets — 115

20.2.1.	Interest Relief	115
20.2.2.	Re-investment Of Capital Gains	116
20.2.3.	Relevant Earnings	116

21. *Tax Tips For Landlords Renovating Properties* 117

21.1. Investment Vs Trading — 117

21.1.1.	Investment Properties	117
21.1.2.	Trading	117
21.1.3.	Property Purchased As A Residence	117
21.1.4.	The Impact Of Intention	118

21.2. Buying The Renovation Property: SDLT — 118

21.3. Relief For The Costs of Doing Up The Property — 118

- 21.3.1. Revenue V Capital Expenditure — 119
- 21.3.2. Repairs – Relief For Revenue Expenses — 119
- 21.3.3. Capital Expenditure — 119
- 21.3.4. Extensive Alterations To The Property — 120
- 21.3.5. Repairs To A Dilapidated Property – The Capital Expenditure Trap — 120
- 21.3.6. Splitting Expenditure Between Capital and Revenue — 120
- 21.3.7. Relief For Capital Expenditure – Cash Basis — 120
- 21.3.8. Relief For Capital Expenditure – Accruals Basis — 121
- 21.3.9. Relief For Capital Expenditure – Capital Gains — 121
- 21.3.10. Relief For Pre-Letting Expenditure — 121
- 21.3.11. Work Undertaken While Rental Property Is Empty — 122

21.4. VAT — 122

21.5. Selling The Property — 122

- 21.5.1. Selling An Investment Property — 122
- 21.5.2. Property Development – Taxing the Profit On Sale — 123
- 21.5.3. Selling The Main Residence — 123

21.6. Converting A Property Into Flats - Case Studies — 123

- 21.6.1. Case Study 1 – House Converted By A Developer Into Flats For Sale — 123
- 21.6.2. Case Study 2 – Landlord Converts Rental Property To Flats For Let — 124
- 21.6.3. Case Study 3 – Homeowner Converts House To Flats Prior To Sale — 125
- 21.6.4. Case Study 4 – House Converted Into Flats, One Sold, One Lived In As A Home — 126

22. Understanding Capital Gains Tax (CGT) — 128

22.1. When You Are Liable To Pay CGT — 128

22.2. How Your CGT Bill Is Calculated — 129

23. Reporting And Tax Payment Changes From 6th April 2020 — 131

23.1. When May A Residential Property Gain Arise? — 131

23.2. Higher Tax Rates For Residential Property Gains — 131

23.3. Reporting Pre-6 April 2020 Residential Property Gains — 131

23.4. New Rules From 6 April 2020 — 132

23.5. Requirement To Make A Payment On Account — 132

23.6. Calculating The Payment On Account — 132

23.7. Finalising The Position — 133

24. Private Residence Relief (PPR) — 134

24.1. What Is Private Residence Relief? — 134

- 24.1.1. Full Residence Relief — 134
- 24.1.2. Partial Residence Relief — 135

24.2. How Long In A Property Before It Can Be Classed As My PPR? — 135

24.3. More Insight Into What Makes A PPR — 136

  24.3.1. Practical Tip... 137

 24.4. **Private Residence CGT Exemption - How To Lose It!** _____ 137

 24.5. **Private Residence Relief – When Relief May Be Restricted** _____ 138

  24.5.1. Restriction 1 – Use For Purpose Of A Trade, Business Profession Or Vocation 139
  24.5.2. Restriction 2 – Change Of Use.. 140
  24.5.3. Restriction 3 – Development Gains.. 140

25. *Increasing Property Value And Avoiding Tax*... *142*

 25.1. **No CGT On The First 24 Months Of Ownership** _____ 142

26. *Nominating Residence To Avoid CGT*.. *144*

 26.1. **Having More Than One Family Home** _____ 144

 26.2. **Nominating Your Residence to HMRC** _____ 144

27. *Other Ways To Reduce Your CGT Bill*.. *146*

 27.1. **Using Your Annual CGT Allowance** _____ 146

 27.2. **Capital Losses** _____ 147

 27.3. **Buying And Selling Costs** _____ 148

 27.4. **Selling At The Right Time Can Save You Tax!** _____ 148

28. *Advanced Strategies For Avoiding CGT*.. *150*

 28.1. **How To Claim An Additional Three Years Of PPR** _____ 150

 28.2. **Claiming PPR When Working Overseas** _____ 151

 28.3. **Claiming PPR When Re-locating In The UK** _____ 151

 28.4. **CGT Implications Of Providing Property To Dependent Relatives** _____ 152

29. *Inheritance Tax Considerations For Landlords* *153*

 29.1. **Introduction To IHT Considerations** _____ 153

 29.2. **Nature of IHT** _____ 153

  29.2.1. Nil Rate Band.. 153
  29.2.2. Transferable Nil Rate Band 153
  29.2.3. Case Study 1; Transferable Nil Rate Band 154
  29.2.4. Residence Nil Rate Band 154
  29.2.5. Exemption For Gifts To Spouses And Civil Partners.. 155
  29.2.6. Potentially Exempt Transfers... 155
  29.2.7. Gifts Out Of Income.. 156
  29.2.8. Annual Exemption 156
  29.2.9. Other Exempt Gifts 156
  29.2.10. Business Property Relief.. 157
  29.2.11. Agricultural Relief 157
  29.2.12. Making Use Of Exemptions And Relief... 158

 29.3. **Benefits Of Making A Will** _____ 158

29.3.1.	Intestacy Provisions	158
29.3.2.	Surviving spouse or civil partner and surviving children	158
29.3.3.	Surviving spouse or civil partner but no children	159
29.3.4.	No Surviving Spouse Or Civil Partner But Children	159
29.3.5.	No Surviving Spouse, Civil Partner or Issue	159
29.3.6.	No Living Relatives	159
29.3.7.	Case Study 2 – Operation Of The Intestacy Rules	159
29.3.8.	Post-Death Variation	160
29.3.9.	Case Study 3 - Post-Death Variation	160

29.4. Jointly Owned Property — 161

29.4.1.	Joint Tenants	161
29.4.2.	Tenants in Common	161

29.5. Making Use Of The Nil Rate Bands — 162

29.5.1.	Leave Property Valued Up To £325,000 Other Than To A Spouse / Civil Partner	162
29.5.2.	Case Study 4 – Utilise The Nil Rate Band	163
29.5.3.	Don't Waste The RNRB	163

29.6. Make Lifetime Gifts — 163

29.6.1.	Gifts And CGT	163
29.6.2.	Case Study 5 – CGT Gift Trap	164
29.6.3.	Potential Double Charge	164
29.6.4.	Case Study 6 – IHT and CGT Trap	164
29.6.5.	Beware The Gifts With Reservation Rules	164
29.6.6.	Pre-Owned Assets Rules	165

29.7. Is BPR Available? — 165

29.8. Consider A Trust — 165

29.8.1.	Discretionary Trust	165
29.8.2.	Nil Rate Band Trust	166

29.9. Property Companies And Growth Shares — 166

29.10. Providing For The IHT Bill — 166

29.10.1.	Make Gifts From Income	166
29.10.2.	Take Out A Whole Life Policy	167

30. *How To Better Manage Your Landlord Taxes* *168*

1. About The Authors

Some words about the authors of this unique guide, bringing together UK tax specialists and a property investor!

1.1. Sarah Bradford – Tax Specialist

Sarah Bradford BA (Hons) FCA CTA (Fellow) is a director of Writetax Ltd, a company providing technical writing services on tax and National Insurance.

Sarah writes widely on tax and contributes to a number of newsletters, books and reports available through the **TaxInsider.co.uk** website. These include:

- Business Tax Insider;
- Property Tax Insider;
- Tax Insider Professional;

1.2. Arthur Weller - Tax Specialist

Arthur Weller (CTA) is a tax specialist who advises other accountants. He is one of the most knowledgeable and respected tax specialists in the country.

He is also the lead technical tax specialist and design consultant for www.property-tax-portal.co.uk.

Arthur is based in the northwest and qualified in 1997 as a certified accountant in a small firm of accountants. They specialised to a degree in property, and he worked for some years in their tax department.

He then moved on to a medium-sized firm, where he was the technical manager in the tax department.

In 1998 he passed the exams of the Institute of Taxation, and in June 2000 he left to set up his own tax consultancy.

Arthur works mainly in an advisory capacity for accountants in all areas of taxation. He also runs a telephone help line, giving phone advice on all areas of taxation to accountants around the country.

Much of his work has been focused in the following areas:

- property taxation (Arthur is regarded as a property tax specialist);
- capital gains tax;
- stamp duty;
- income tax;
- company tax;

Arthur has advised over 2,000 landlords, property investors and tax professionals through the Property Tax Portal Consultancy page here:

>> https://www.property-tax-portal.co.uk/consultancy_arthur.shtml

1.3. Amer Siddiq - The Landlord

First and foremost, Amer Siddiq is a UK landlord/property investor. He is passionate about all aspects of property investment and over the last nine years has grown a portfolio in the northwest of England

As well as growing a portfolio and speaking in public at various property investment events, Amer has also brought to market a number of websites to help landlords to better manage and grow their portfolios whilst reducing their taxes.
These include:

landlord vision	**Landlord Vision** Our next generation landlord software solution that runs in the cloud. **Take your FREE Trial today.** Visit: www.landlordvision.co.uk
tax insider	**Tax Insider** A website providing monthly tax newsletters to help UK taxpayers minimise their taxes. Visit: www.taxinsider.co.uk

1.4. Acknowledgements

Lee Sharpe, Chartered Tax Advisor and author of:

- How to Use Companies to Reduce Property Taxes,
- Tax Secrets for Property Developers and Renovators

Both books can be purchased through www.property-tax-portal.co.uk website.

Lee is also a public speaker and provides valuable tax expertise to the www.property-tax-portal.co.uk and www.taxinsider.co.uk websites.

Other acknowledgements include:
- Mark McLaughlin CTA (Fellow) ATT (Fellow) TEP
- Jennifer Adams FCIS TEP ATT (Fellow)- Principal
- Alan Pink FCA CTA

2. The Importance Of Tax Planning

We all instinctively do some tax planning in our daily lives, even if it is simply remembering to buy our "duty frees" when we return from our holiday abroad.

If you are going to make the best of your property business, then you need to be alert to the tax implications of your business plans, and to any opportunities to reduce the likely tax bill. Your instinct may be enough for your duty-free goodies, but for tax on your business, you need a more structured approach!

"Tax planning" means arranging your business affairs so that you pay the minimum amount of tax that the law requires. It does not mean trying to conceal things from the Taxman, and it does not mean indulging in highly complex (and expensive!) artificial "tax avoidance" schemes.

"Every man is entitled if he can to order his affairs so that the tax attaching under the appropriate Acts is less than it would otherwise be." That is what the House of Lords said in 1935, when they found for the Duke of Westminster and against the Inland Revenue. This still holds true today, though there is now a mass of "anti-avoidance" legislation to consider when thinking about tax planning – and before you ask, the Duke's tax planning idea was stopped by anti-avoidance legislation!

2.1. Knowing When To Consider Planning

A question you will most certainly ask yourself is 'when should I consider tax planning for my property business?'

The short answer is "all the time", but to be realistic, no-one is likely to do this. The trick is to develop by experience, a sense of when a tax planning opportunity (or a potentially expensive tax pitfall) is likely to present itself.

You should consider tax planning in all of the following situations, for example:

2.1.1. Buying

If you are buying a property, you need to consider:

- Buying the property – It could be you as an individual, you and your spouse, you and a business partner, a Limited Company owned by you, or perhaps a Trust you have set up. Your decision will depend on your future business strategy

- Financing the property – You will need to consider whether you are taking out a mortgage, and if so how will it be secured. It may not always make sense to secure the loan on the property you are buying if you have other assets on which you can secure the loan.

- Plans for the property – It could be that you are you buying the property to sell it again in the short term, or to hold it long term and benefit from the rental income. The tax treatment will be different according to which is the case, and different planning should be done before the property is bought.

2.1.2. Repairs And Refurbishment

If you spend money on a property, you need to consider:

- Whether you are doing it in order to sell it again in the short term, or whether you will continue letting it.

- If the work being done is classed as a **repair** to the property, or an **improvement.** See icon below for the difference between the two.

  The distinction between a repair and an improvement to a property is very important, because although the cost of repairs can be deducted from your rental income for tax purposes, an improvement can only be claimed as a deduction against CGT when you sell the property.

  Essentially, a repair is when you replace like with like, whereas an improvement involves adding to the property (say, a conservatory or a loft conversion), or replacing something with something significantly better (say, removing the old storage heaters and installing oil-fired central heating).

  HMRC do not always behave logically when it comes to repairs versus improvements.

  James Bailey shares the following experience with us:

  "A client of mine sold a seaside property, in circumstances where he would have to pay CGT on the sale profit. He had spent a lot of money on this property, which when he bought it had not been touched since the early 1950s.

  He had ripped out the old "utility" kitchen, for example, and replaced it with a state-of –the –art designer affair in gleaming slate, chrome, and steel. The old 1950s cooker had had some Bakelite knobs to turn the gas on and off – the new kitchen range had the computer power of the average 1970s space capsule.

  Clearly an improvement, and so deductible from his capital gain, but HMRC tried to argue that one kitchen is much like another and he was just replacing like with like – so they said it was a repair, which was no good to him in his case as there was no rental income from which he could deduct the cost of repairs."

2.1.3. Selling

When you decide to dispose of a property, there are other tax issues to consider:

- Who is the property going to? – If it is to someone "connected" with you, such as a close relative or a business partner, and if you do not charge them the full market value, HMRC can step in and tax you as if you had sold it for full value.

- Will you be paying CGT or income tax on the profit you make? – The planning opportunities are very different, depending on which tax is involved.

- What are the terms of the sale? Is it just a cash sale, or is the buyer a developer who is offering you a "slice of the action" in the form of a share of the profits from the development? There is important anti-avoidance legislation to consider if this is the case.

2.1.4. Life Changes

Whenever your life undergoes some significant changes, you should consider tax planning.

Here are some examples when tax planning should be considered:

- Getting married – a married couple (and a civil partnership) have a number of tax planning opportunities denied to single people, but there are also one or two pitfalls to watch out for.

- Moving house – it is usually not a good idea to sell the old house immediately, as there are often tax advantages to keeping it and letting it out.

- Changing your job. You may become a higher or lower rate taxpayer, and this may mean you should change your tax strategy.

  If you are moving house, and you sell the old residence, you will have the cash left after you have paid off the mortgage and the various removal costs to spend on your new home. If you need a mortgage to buy the new home, the interest on that mortgage is not allowed as a deduction for tax purposes.

  If, instead, you remortgage the old house and let it out, ALL the mortgage interest you pay can be deducted against the rent you receive (subject to the 2017 rules for interest paid by residential landlords) whatever you do with the cash you have released – and you may well be able to sell the house after nine months of letting (or sometimes a longer period), and pay no CGT on the increased value since you stopped living there.

- Death – IHT is charged at 40% on the value of your estate when you die, to the extent that the value is greater than (for 2024/25) £325,000. By planning early enough it is possible to reduce the IHT burden considerably.

2.1.5. Politics

There are two occasions each year when you need to be particularly alert – the Budget Report in the Autumn, and The Spring Statement in March.

On both these occasions the Chancellor of the Exchequer announces tax rates, and new tax legislation, which might well affect you and your property business. In some cases, however, new tax legislation is announced at other times – it pays to keep a weather eye on the financial pages of the newspaper, or to subscribe to a magazine or journal that will alert you to important tax changes that may affect your business.

2.1.6. End And Start Of The Tax Year

The tax year ends on the 5th April each year and it is a good idea to review your tax situation before this date to make sure you are not missing any planning opportunities.

2.2. The Real Benefits Of Tax Planning

Robert Kiyosaki, author of the number one bestselling book 'Rich Dad Poor Dad', says *'Every time people try to punish the rich, the rich don't simply comply, they react. They have the money, power and intent to change things. They do not sit there and voluntarily pay more taxes. They search for ways to minimize their tax burden'.*

The whole purpose of tax planning is to save you tax and to put more profits in your pocket. That is why the rich are always looking at ways of beating the taxman, because they benefit from tax planning.

2.2.1. Paying Less Tax

When I (co-author Amer) started investing in property the challenge to me was not to just grow a property portfolio but to grow it in the most tax efficient way possible.

It soon dawned on me that implementing just the simplest of tax saving strategies was going to help me to make considerably more profits.

Don't fall into the trap where you only think about tax when you are considering selling or even worse after you have sold the property.

By taking tax advice at the right times and on a regular basis you will legitimately avoid or reduce taxes both in the short and the long term.

This means that you will have greater profits to spend as you wish.

2.2.2. Clear 'Entrance' And 'Exit' Strategies

When you sit down and analyse properties that you are considering for investment, you will no doubt look at how much rental income the property will generate and what you expect to achieve in capital appreciation.

Knowing the estimated tax liabilities right from the outset will save you from any nasty surprises in the future.

> Your personal circumstances can change at a whim. The last thing that you want to do is fall into a situation where you are forced to sell a property but are unable to pay the taxman because you never considered your tax situation.

2.2.3. Staying Focused

When you are deciding on the property investment strategies that you are going to adopt it is a good idea to talk them through with a tax adviser.

If your investment strategy changes then it is likely to have an impact on your tax strategy, so it should be reviewed with your tax adviser.

Your tax strategy will go hand in hand with your investment strategy and will help you to keep focused on your property investment and financial goals.

2.2.4. Improving Cash Flow

One of the challenges that you will face as a property investor is cash flow. In other words, you need to make sure that you have enough money coming in from your property business to pay for all property related bills, maintenance and repairs, and of course tax on the rental profits.

> Remember, timing of expenditures can be the difference between a 'high' and a 'nil' tax bill. Therefore, keeping in regular contact with your tax adviser, especially when coming towards the end of the tax year can have a significant impact on your property cash flow.

2.2.5. Avoiding Common Tax Traps

There are many tax traps that you can fall into if you have not taken any tax advice at all, not to mention the numerous great tax planning opportunities you will miss out on too. It is not uncommon to hear stories about investors who have made a £100,000 profit on a single property and then sold it without taking any tax advice whatsoever. If you fall into this situation, then you could be hit with a hefty tax bill.

It will hurt you even more if after selling you realise that you could have easily turned the tax liability to zero had you taken some simple tax advice.

Good tax advisers will know of the most common traps that you are likely to fall into, so a few minutes spent wisely could save you thousands in taxes.

2.3. Asking HMRC For Tax Advice

From time to time people tell the TaxInsider.co.uk office that all the effort that goes into offering them tax advice is a waste of time, and tax consultants are also unnecessary, because you can simply telephone HM Revenue & Customs (HMRC) and get free advice. However, free advice is not always the best advice.

2.3.1. Making Use Of HMRC Services

Getting advice from HMRC in some circumstances is always a good idea – for example, they operate a number of "clearance" services whereby you can set out the details of a proposed transaction for them, and they will tell you the tax consequences they believe will flow from it.

Some of these clearances are enshrined in statute – there are some quite draconian examples of anti-avoidance legislation which can also catch quite innocent commercial transactions, and there is a statutory process for obtaining HMRC's agreement in advance that they will not wheel out their sledgehammers to crack your innocent commercial nut.

There are also other informal HMRC clearance procedures which can be useful when you are considering a transaction where the tax treatment may turn on a matter of opinion, and it is useful to know HMRC's opinion in advance.

It is also possible to agree valuations of assets for capital gains tax purposes where these are needed to complete a tax return – much better to have the discussion before you put the return in than to hope for the best and submit it, only to have the same discussion as part of an HMRC "Aspect Enquiry" where the possibility of penalties looms if they consider your valuation was a little sloppy!

Tax specialists use such services frequently on behalf of clients, and they are a great help in providing a better service for them.

2.3.2. The Drawback

However, the "help" that the people who contact Tax Insider are referring to is the "help" you can get by ringing HMRC up while filling in your tax return, or when confronted by a tax situation that you do not understand. In some cases, no harm will result, and you may even get the right answer, but on the whole professional advisors are very nervous about this "do it yourself" approach to tax.

HMRC's own policy on giving advice is contained in their "Code of Practice 10", and the following sentence from that document illustrates a major gap in their service:

"However, we will not help with tax planning, or advise on transactions designed to avoid or reduce the tax charge which might otherwise be expected to arise".

2.3.3. Practical Tip

There is a serious point here – HMRC do their best to promote the view that there is a "correct" amount of tax that is due as a result of any particular transaction, whereas in all but the simplest of cases, there are grey areas and the way a transaction is structured can make a big difference to the resulting tax bill.

As Lord Tomlin said in the House of Lords during the case of The Duke of Westminster v The Commissioners of Inland Revenue in 1936 ***"Every man is entitled if he can to order his affairs so that the tax attaching under the appropriate Acts is less than it would otherwise be"***.

That remains good law and seems to me a sensible way to deal with the State's demands for ever higher taxes, but don't expect HMRC to help you!

3. Making Tax Digital For Landlords

On 18 March 2015 under the heading of 'Making Tax Easier', the then Chancellor, George Osborne, announced that the chore of submitting annual self-assessment tax returns by 31 January was to be abolished. There were loud cheers from back benchers but eight years have passed and we are still submitting annual returns.

The initiative has been titled 'Making Tax Digital' (MTD) and is one of the most significant changes to be made to the UK tax system in generations. It will affect all taxpayers, including landlords. Various reasons have been put forward for the delay in implementation including the pandemic but a recent announcement confirmed deferment until 6 April 2026.

3.1. What Is Making Tax Digital?

The two key requirements for MTD are to:

- keep transaction records via a 'digital link' and
- use compatible software to submit returns to HMRC

HMRC are looking for 'transparency' between the underlying accounting records of the business and tax returns; this, HMRC believes, will reduce the risk of tax error, making compliance and enforcement more efficient.

Under the MTD system, the method of tax return submission will change. Paper returns will no longer be permitted nor will taxpayers be able to submit online via their Government Gateway account. Instead, transactions will be recorded digitally and the detail submitted using specific MTD compatible software. The software will electronically link bookkeeping records into HMRC's MTD computers.

Importantly, HMRC will not provide software to enable submissions and landlords will be compelled to use commercially produced software. Spreadsheets will still be permitted and if used, the initial input of data will be keyed in manually. Further transfer, capture or modification of that same data will be by special software (termed 'bridging' software). That same software will submit the information to HMRC directly. Software will need to be purchased whether spreadsheets are the chosen option or not.

NOTE: Landlord Vision is recognised by HMRC as being fully compliant MTD software and that has been written especially for landlords.

3.2. What Will Stay The Same?

No changes are being made to:

- the underlying tax rules;
- the level of detail of information and headings, which will remain the same as the current self-assessment tax return, or
- the current payment deadlines for income tax.

However, there will be changes to the number of returns (termed 'updates') submitted and the submission dates.

3.3. Submission Dates

The annual tax return submitted every year by 31 January is to be abolished. Instead, taxpayers will be required to submit 'updates' every quarter (or more frequently if the taxpayer so wishes). The time frame for submission will be from 10 days before the quarter end to precisely one month from the end of each quarter.

An 'end of period statement' will also be required by 31 January after the year end confirming the previous submissions' data, including claims such as the restriction of mortgage interest, (if such information has not already been included in the 'updates') and other taxable income (e.g. investment and employment income). A 'Finalisation statement' will pull all 'updates' together to calculate the final tax due.

3.3.1. Number Of Submissions

MTD regulations state that individual landlords will be required to submit quarterly 'updates' for each property business category i.e. separate 'updates' for lettings, furnished holiday lets and overseas lets. The minimum number of submissions will be five per tax year but depending upon the taxpayers' type and income level there could be as many as 20 as the example shows.

Example

Julian is a self-employed builder whose yearend is 30 April. He is registered for VAT and submits his VAT returns for the quarters to the end of April, July, October and January. He is also a landlord with two residential properties, one being furnished holiday accommodation.

Julian will need to submit:

- a quarterly MTD 'update' for each of his two property businesses (8);
- a quarterly MTD 'update' for his building trade (4);
- an 'End of period statement' for each of those three businesses (3);
- four VAT returns (4);

and

- a finalisation statement (1);

– a total of **20 reports** for each tax year.

3.3.2. 'Real Time Basis'

When an 'update' is submitted, HMRC's computer will calculate the taxpayer's potential tax bill as close to 'real time' as possible and at the same time remind (termed 'prompt') the taxpayer as to the dates of payment - the idea being that this will aid taxpayers to put aside monies towards the final tax bill, pay the correct amount of tax, putting a stop to underpayments or overpayments.

As part of the initiative it is intended for there to be an online digital account similar to how accounts are viewed on a bank screen online. This digital account will enable taxpayers to view and manage their tax information in one place including their current ('real time') tax liabilities whichever type of tax is paid. Eventually taxpayers will have the ability to offset overpayments of one tax against underpayments of others.

3.4. When Is MTD Starting?

3.4.1. Stage 1

MTD is being introduced in stages. All VAT registered businesses (including those furnished holiday let businesses subject to VAT) had to be registered for 'Making Tax Digital for VAT' by 1 April 2022.

3.4.2. Stages 2 And 3

The timetable for MTD for income tax has been amended several times. However, it has now been confirmed that (barring any further delays or problems with HMRC's systems), as MTD will apply to all self-employed, partnerships and landlords (including trusts which receive income from property) whose annual business or property income exceeds £50,000 as from 6 April 2026. Individuals with annual business or property income greater than £30,000 will be brought into the system a year later on 6 April 2027.

3.4.3. Which Landlords Will Be Affected?

Landlords with less than £30,000 annual income will be exempt - everyone else will have no choice but to comply. The income figure is the income from all properties, not just the profit figure. For landlords who are both self-employed and receive rental income the amount is from all sources of such income combined. Income from employment will not count.

Certain exemptions may be made for those taxpayers unable to use digital tools due to their religion, age or disability. There is also likely to be an exemption for those affected by low internet speeds (under 2 mb/s).

3.5. MTD Compliance

3.5.1. All Landlords

Although there will be no requirement to submit actual invoices or receipts, this back up information must still be retained. Eventually HMRC would like taxpayers to use software sophisticated enough to scan receipts so the details are loaded automatically into the chosen software. They believe that this method of 'capture' will reduce the need for manual loading (and as such 'mistakes') and the time incurred in creating quarterly submissions. However, such sophisticated software costs and HMRC have backed away from insisting that this type of software be used.

Submissions will be of total figures only and the headings will be the same standard expense headings already in use on the Property pages of the current tax return.

3.5.2. Practical Tip

Many landlords use their personal current account to collect rents and pay expenses. It is suggested that landlords apply for a separate bank account over the next year to hold these figures in one place and make analysing expenses easier. The account need not be a business account but can be an ordinary personal current account.

3.5.3. Multiple Properties

Where multiple properties are held within a property business, rental income and expenditure will be recorded for the business as a whole rather than shown per individual property. However, should information be received from third parties (e.g. letting agents) summaries, those figures can be entered into the software as a single invoice.

3.5.4. Jointly Owned Properties

Currently, each individual provides information on their own tax return detailing their share of the rental income and allowable expenses. This procedure will remain where a property is jointly owned, each individual being required to keep digital records for their share of income and expenditure.

3.5.5. How And When Will Tax Payments Be Made?

HMRC currently plans to retain the dates by which payments must be made, namely on 31 January and 31 July as required. However, voluntary payments will also be permitted at the discretion and interval of the taxpayer's choosing.

Hidden in the Budget consultation published on 23 March 2021 is a sentence which possibly is the real reason for MTD:

"The government is publishing a call for evidence to begin to explore the opportunities and challenges of more frequent payment of income tax within Income Tax Self-Assessment ...based on in-year information'.

3.6. The New System Of Penalties

Alongside the introduction of MTD, HMRC announced a new penalty regime. The regime is currently levied on VAT registered businesses and will also apply to MTD for Income Tax when it begins from April 2026 and possibly MTD for Corporation Tax when implemented.

3.6.1. Late Submission

- Taxpayers will receive one point for every missed submission deadline; HMRC will notify the taxpayer of each point as incurred. The points will expire after two years
- When a taxpayer reaches a certain threshold a financial penalty of £200 will be charged; this threshold will be four points for landlords making quarterly submissions.

- Once the threshold has been reached, the taxpayer will be required to bring all outstanding returns from the preceding 24 months up to date and achieve the period of compliance for the following 12 months for the points to be reset to zero.
- Points will be totalled separately for different submission obligations i.e. should a taxpayer be required to make both self-employed and landlord submissions the points system is separate.

3.6.2. Late Payment Regime

Taxpayers will no longer receive an automatic penalty if they fail to meet a submission obligation, but instead incur a penalty point for each failure as follows:

- no penalty if the outstanding tax is paid within 15 days after the due date
- after 15 days, a penalty of 2% of any outstanding tax will be applied
- this increases to 4% of any outstanding tax if still unpaid 31 days after the tax was due to be paid.

3.6.3. First Year

HMRC have confirmed that for the first year of implementation a 'light touch' approach to applying the first penalty (i.e. 2% after 15 days) will be made. Taxpayers will be allowed 30 days to approach HMRC to ask for a 'Time to pay' arrangement. The 4% penalty will be charged on any outstanding tax remaining unpaid after the 30 days even if an arrangement has been made.

3.7. Simplified 'Cash Basis' For Unincorporated Property Businesses

As part of the changes, the method by which unincorporated property businesses account for their property income has changed. These changes make the 'cash basis' of accounting the default option where receipts of that business are less than £150,000 (unless the business elects to use the 'accruals basis').

The 'cash basis' is used to account for income and expenses when the income is received and expenses are paid. The current general disallowance of capital expenditure under the 'cash basis' is replaced by a more specific disallowance for certain assets. The 'accruals basis' accounts for income over the period to which it relates and for expenses in the period for which the liability is incurred.

3.8. Possible Timetable For 2026/27 And 2027/8

For landlords who do not have any other self-employed or partnership income the deadlines for each submission for the first year 2026/27 will be:

1. 1st 'update' 2026/27 - submit June 2026
2. 2nd 'update' 2026/27 - submit Sept 2026
3. 3rd 'update' 2026/27 - submit Dec 2026
4. 2025/26 Self-Assessment tax return - submit by 31 January 2027
5. 4th 'update' 2026/27 - submit March 2027

6. 1st 'update' 2027/28 - submit June 2027
7. 2nd 'update' 2027/28 - submit Sept 2027
8. 3rd 'update' 2027/28 - submit Dec 2027
9. 5th and final 'end of year activity' 2026/27 - submit 31 January 2027

3.9. Final Points

Over time the information submitted under MTD will create a picture of a taxpayer's business, which HMRC believes will enable more accurate comparisons with other similar businesses than are currently available. This can only mean more targeted enquiries and, as indicated above, eventually enable more regular tax payments.

April 2026 may seem a long way in the future however the delay in implementation has given all affected landlords further time to prepare. As such it will be prudent for landlords to be aware of the changes and put procedures in place to ensure that the transition from the 'old' system to the 'new' goes as smoothly as possible in the circumstances.

3.10. Invest In Landlord Software

Landlord vision is a cloud-based property management software for busy landlords who need to manage the essential administration of their property and finances quickly and efficiently.

Visit: www.landlordvision.co.uk

landlord vision

Knowing Your Property Tax Strategy

4. Understanding Your Tax Liabilities

Over the past few years property investment has become a very profitable way to make money.

Unfortunately, there are very few people who consider the tax implications of their investment strategy before they decide to invest. Instead they take a view that they will address the tax issues when they decide to dispose of the property. This can be a very costly mistake as some simple planning can help to avoid large tax bills in the future.

The table below gives an indication of the tax that may be due if you follow any of the popular strategies outlined below.

Strategy	Description	Income Tax	Capital Gains Tax
Buy-to-let	Probably the most popular investment method and a strategy for long-term investment. Income tax will be due on the annual rental profits and CGT due when the property is disposed of.	Yes	Yes
Develop & Sell	This is typically classed as a short-term (i.e. 3-6 months) investment and only Income Tax is due if you are trading in properties in this way. All property development related expenditures can be offset against the final selling price.	Yes	No
Develop & Rent	Another typical long-term investment, where the property is developed and then rented out. All capital expenditure incurred developing the property can be offset when the property is disposed.	Yes	Yes

	However rental profit will be subject to annual income tax.		
Buy & Sell	If you are a master or want to become a master of buying undervalued property and then re-selling at a higher price, then you will be classed as a property trader and will typically be subject to Income Tax only.	Yes	No
Buy-let-live	A good investment strategy to make use of some very significant tax breaks if you are sitting on large capital gains. This strategy only really applies to investors who intent to hold only a small number of properties during their lifetime i.e. (3-6 properties). Again, income tax will be due on rental profits and CGT when the property is disposed of.	Yes	Yes (but is dramatic-ally reduced)
Buy-live-let	Probably the most tax efficient way to avoid capital gains tax for the small investor. This increasingly popular strategy involves letting your previous main residence when buying a new home or moving abroad. Again, income tax will be due on rental profits and CGT when the property is disposed of.	Yes	Yes (but is dramatic-ally reduced)
Rent-a-Room	If you decide to rent-a-room that is part of your main residence then you can receive an annual rental income, to the value of £7,500 and not have any income tax liability. Ay income above this amount will be subject to income tax. CGT is not due if you sell your main residence which has been	Yes (if claiming rent-a-room relief and income is greater than £7,500)	No (if tenants live with the family owning the property)

	classed as your only home during the whole period of ownership. Please Note: if the tenants renting do not live together with the family, then there can be CGT on that part of the house rented out.		
Furnished Holiday Lets	If you let a furnished property as a holiday let, then you will be subject to income tax on any rental profits. There are number of very generous tax breaks available for those investing in Furnished Holiday Lets.	Yes	Yes

How To Slash Your Property Income Tax

Before we look at the different income tax saving strategies, it is important to understand what is meant by the term **income tax** and when property investors and landlords are liable to pay it.

5. Income Tax Liabilities For Investors/Traders

Anybody investing in property is liable to pay income tax on any profitable income that is generated from their properties.

There are two main categories of people who invest in property, and both are liable to pay income tax. The characteristics of each are detailed in the following sections.

5.1. Property Investor

If you invest in property for the long term, i.e., you have buy-to-let properties, then you will be referred to as a **property investor** (more commonly known as a landlord). This is because you are holding on to a property for the long term.

If you are letting your investment properties, then you will be liable to pay income tax annually on the rental profits.

It is also likely that you will have another source of income, unless you have a large portfolio of properties where the rental income funds your lifestyle.

5.2. Property Traders/Dealers

If you are investing in property for the short term, i.e., 6–12 months, and intend to sell with the aim of generating a dealing profit, then you will be referred to as **property dealer** or **property trader**.

Property dealers and traders are liable to pay income tax when they sell the property.

You will find that most full-time property developers or renovators are classed as property dealers/traders.

5.3. Income Tax Rates

You can use the following link to view the income tax rates for previous years:

http://www.hmrc.gov.uk/rates/it.htm

The current rates of income tax for the 2024–2025 tax year are detailed in the table below:

INCOME TAX 2024–2025

Rate	Band	Description
Nil	£0 to £12,570	The first £12,570 of each individual's income is Tax Free.
20%	£12,571 to £50,270	The next £37,700 is taxed at 20%.
40%	£50,271 to £100,000	The next £49,730 is taxed at 40%.
60%	£100,001 to £125,140	The next £25,140 is taxed at 60%. This is because of the withdrawal of the Personal Allowance.
45%	> £125,140	Anything above £125,140 is taxed at 45%

The above table assumes that the personal allowance is £12,570. It also disregards the 0% tax rate on savings income for the first £5,000.

5.4. Income Tax Calculation Case Studies

Here are some case studies to illustrate how the tax liability is calculated for property investors and property dealers/traders.

5.4.1. Income Tax Calculation For Property Investors

The case study below illustrates the income tax liability for a basic-rate taxpayer.

Income Tax Calculation for Property Investor (1)

John works as a local government officer and receives an annual salary of £20,000. He buys a property close to his local hospital for £95,000. He receives a monthly rental income of £600.

The property is let for the whole 2024–2025 tax year, which means that he has received an annual rental income of £7,200.

In the tax year he has also incurred property-related expenses of £1,400.

These expenditures are made up as follows:

Expense	Amount
Insurance	£600
Plumbing (to fix water leak)	£150

Annual gas safety inspection	£100
Central heating maintenance contract	£300
Replacement door fitted	£250
Total Expenditure	£1,400

This means that John's taxable rental profit is £5,800 (i.e., £7,200 − £1,400).

On this amount he is liable to pay tax at 20%. This is because his £5,800 rental profit falls into the basic rate band.

Therefore, his tax liability is **£1,160** on the £5,800 profit.

The following case study illustrates how the rental income from the property pushes John into the higher-rate tax band.

Income Tax Calculation for Property Investor (2)

This is the same scenario as in the previous case study. The only difference is that John has an annual salary of £48,270.

John's tax liability on the £5,800 profit is now calculated as follows.

The first £2,000 is taxed at the basic rate of 20%.

The remaining £3,800 is taxed at the higher rate of 40%. This is because the rental profit has taken his total income into the higher-rate tax band.

Therefore, his tax liability is as follows:

(£2,000 × 0.2) + (£3,800 × 0.4)
£400 + £1,520

= £1,920

John's tax liability is **£1,920** on the £5,800 profit.

5.4.2. Income Tax Calculation For Property Developers

It is important to remember that if you become a property dealer, then this is a new self-employed trade and you are liable for Class 4 National Insurance (NI) on the profits as well as for Class 2 NI. See HMRC leaflet SE1 Thinking of working for yourself:

https://assets.publishing.service.gov.uk/media/5a7df5f0ed915d74e622331a/se1.pdf.

In order to make the case studies in this section easier to understand the NI contributions have not been calculated.

The following case study illustrates how the income tax liability is calculated for a part-time property dealer.

Income Tax Calculation for Property Dealer (1)

Bill works as a local government officer and earns a salary of £30,270. Bill wants to become a property developer, so he buys a run-down property for £50,000 in May 2024.

He spends £20,000 renovating and re-decorating the property before selling it six months later for £95,000.

This gives him a taxable profit of £25,000 (i.e. selling price – (purchase price + costs incurred on the property)).

Bill's tax liability on the £25,000 profit is made in the 2024–2025 tax year, so his tax liability is calculated as follows.

The first £20,000 is taxed at the basic rate of 20%.

The remaining £5,000 is taxed at the higher rate of 40%. This is because the property development profit has taken his total income into the higher-rate tax band.

Therefore, his tax liability is as follows:

(£20,000 × 0.2)	+	(£5,000 × 0.4)
£4,000	+	£2,000
	=	£6,000

Bill's tax liability is **£6,000** on the £25,000 profit.

The following case study illustrates how the income tax liability is calculated for a full-time property dealer.

Income Tax Calculation for Property Dealer (2)

Robert, a colleague of Bill and John, resigns from his job in the local government and decides to become a full-time property dealer.

In his first year of dealing he buys two properties, renovates them, and sells them for a profit of £55,000 each. This means that he has a taxable income of £110,000. The profit is made in the 2024–2025 tax year, so his tax liability is calculated as follows.

- The first £12,570 is tax-free due to the personal allowance.
- The next £37,700 is taxed at the basic rate of 20%.
- The next £49,730 is taxed at the rate of 40%.
- The remaining £10,000 is taxed at the even higher rate of 60%.

Here is the tax calculation:

Tax Rate	Amount	Tax Liability
Nil	£12,570	£0
20%	£37,700	£7,540
40%	£49,730	£19,892
60%	£10,000	£6,000
Total Tax Liability		**£33,432**

Therefore, Robert has a tax liability of **£33,432** on the £110,000 profit.

6. Owning Properties As A Sole Trader

Holding a property in a sole name can be tax beneficial under certain circumstances.

In this section we will get to grips with why people hold properties as a sole trader and will learn about some of the tax benefits and drawbacks of owning properties in this way.

6.1. Buying Properties As A Sole Trader

A **sole trader** is an individual who buys properties in his or her sole name.

Although it is still a very common way to purchase properties, it is not necessarily the most tax efficient.

In most cases, properties are usually purchased as a sole trader for non-tax-related reasons.

Here are the two most common non-tax-related reasons why you might decide to buy property as a sole trader.

a) You don't have a partner who you can invest with.

b) You don't want to invest with anybody else; that is, you can't trust anybody, or you want total control over your investment.

If you have invested for either of these reasons, then you can still make tax savings.

6.2. When Is It Tax Efficient To Buy Property As A Sole Trader?

The ideal scenario for buying a property as a sole trader is if you have no other income.

The reason for this is because you can utilise your annual, tax-free personal allowance.

In simple terms, the further your income is from the higher-rate tax bands, the more you will save in income tax by having the property in your sole name. This is especially true if your partner is a higher-rate taxpayer.

The following two case studies illustrate these points.

Sole Trader With No Income

Joanne is a married woman but does not work. Her husband is a high-flying executive who earns £70,000 per annum.

Upon the death of a relative, Joanne is left £100,000. She uses the entirety of this inheritance to purchase an investment property.

She makes £600 rental profit per month. (She bought the property with cash, so therefore she has no outstanding mortgage or other costs in the tax year).

> This means that she makes an annual rental profit of £7,200.
>
> She is not liable to pay any tax on this amount as it is within the annual personal income tax allowance of £12,570.

Had Joanne bought the property in joint ownership with her husband, then he would have been liable to pay tax at 40% on his share of the investment. If his share of the property was 50%, then he would have an annual tax liability of £1,440.

This means that over a 10-year period, Joanne will see a minimum tax saving of £14,400 by owning the property in her sole name.

> **Property Investor With No Income, but Partner Works**
>
> Chris is married and earns £15,000 per annum as a store sales assistant. His wife runs a pharmacy and earns £45,000 per annum.
>
> They decide that they want to start investing in property and purchase a property for £45,000.
>
> They take tax advice before investing and are told that they will pay less annual income tax if the property is purchased in Chris's sole name.
>
> This is because he is not a higher-rate taxpayer.

6.3. When Is It NOT Tax Efficient To Buy Property As A Sole Trader?

Try not to buy property as a sole trader if you are a higher-rate taxpayer i.e. paying tax at 40%, 45% or even 60%, especially if you can invest with a partner who is a lower-rate taxpayer.

If you are a higher-rate taxpayer, then you will have to pay income tax on any rental income at the higher rate as well.

It would be very poor tax planning on your end if you ended up paying 40%, 45% or 60% tax on all rental income, especially if you had a partner who could make use of the nil rate band or the 20% tax band.

6.4. A Note About Selling Properties When Operating As A Sole Trader

You now know when it is beneficial to buy properties as a sole trader.

However, it is generally better to have a property in a joint name when you come to sell the property.

7. Legal v Beneficial Ownership: A 'Taxing' Distinction!

7.1. Legal And Beneficial Ownership

The two types of ownership are not mutually exclusive, but essentially describe different aspects of property ownership.

While the beneficial owner may often also be the legal owner, (and *vice versa*), this will not always be the case:

- the legal owner is the 'official' or 'formal' owner of the land/property; and
- the beneficial owner is the person with the right to use/occupy the property (without paying for it) and the right to enjoy any income, etc. derived from the property.

A person can be both the legal and beneficial owner of property, at the same time – this is very common.

7.2. Legal Ownership

Legal ownership reflects who is responsible for the land/property. The parties registered under the Land Registry are the legal owners. Under English law, no more than four persons can be formally registered as the legal owners of a parcel of land/property. Those (up to) four persons are essentially equal.

7.3. Beneficial Ownership

The beneficial ownership or 'equitable interest' in property reflects who is entitled to the benefits or fruit of the land, be it in monetary or other form. The law of equity has developed to ensure that fair outcomes are achieved.

> **Example: Ownership Of A Holiday Home**
>
> Bill and Ted put up the funds to buy a holiday home in York. For whatever reason, only Bill's name is noted in the Land Registry. Bill is the legal owner, but Ted is not too bothered by this because he knows that the law of equity will recognise that he is a co-owner and that both Ted and Bill have a beneficial interest in that property.
>
> Furthermore, if Ted put up 2/3rds of the money for the property – i.e. twice Bill's contribution – then the principles of equity will presume that Ted has a greater interest in the property than Bill.
>
> So, if at some future date Bill and Ted's holiday home should be levelled to make way for York's new airport, it will be only equitable to assume that Ted's greater investment at the outset will result in Ted having more of the compensation received.

7.4. Analogies

One way to look at the distinction between legal and beneficial ownership is to consider a limited company:

- the company has owners – its shareholders. If the company's value increases significantly, so does the value of each shareholder's interest in the company. The shareholders are broadly equivalent to the beneficial owners of land. If the company is sold or liquidated, the shareholders get the proceeds; and
- the company also has official custodians/guardians – principally, its directors. The directors have duties both to the shareholders and to others. If a legal claim is made against the company, it is primarily the directors' responsibility to deal with it on behalf of the shareholders. The company directors are broadly equivalent to the legal owners of land.

It is, of course, very common for directors also to be shareholders – there can be an overlap between the legal responsibility, and the beneficial owners.

Another way to look at the distinction is in terms of trusts. For example, In English law, a child cannot take full legal ownership of land until reaching the age of 18. If a deceased parent's will leaves the family home to a young child, a trustee is appointed to look after the property until the child reaches 18 years old. The trustee(s) will be the legal owner(s), whereas the child is the beneficial owner and:

- he or she may live in it – a right to enjoy or occupy the asset; and
- if the property is rented out instead, the child has the right to any income received; and
- if the property is sold, then the proceeds 'belong' to the child.

7.5. Tax Implications

Tax is first and foremost about money. It follows that tax is primarily concerned with who has the beneficial interest in the property, in terms of:

(a) who has a right to the income – income tax follows who receives the income (or is entitled to any income arising);

(b) who has a right to the proceeds of any property disposal or part-disposal – capital gains tax (CGT) will be charged on whoever is entitled to the proceeds as beneficial owner; and

(c) who has a right to enjoy or occupy the property – inheritance tax (IHT) will also follow whoever enjoys the use of the asset (see also 'Tax complications' below).

Stamp duty land tax (SDLT) is more complex and that is perhaps understandable, given its origins. It can potentially apply to transfers of either beneficial or legal ownership. This is a complex area, but it is worth noting that SDLT generally applies only where the value of the interest transferred is at least £40,000.

7.6. Tax Complications

7.6.1. Income Tax

While tax generally follows who is entitled to the income, it can also follow who receives the income (albeit generally as a first step).

For example, trustees sometimes have to file tax returns and pay tax on the money they receive on trust assets, even though it will, ultimately, be paid out to the trust's income beneficiaries. But the trustees are effectively paying the tax 'up front' for the income beneficiaries, who get credit on their own tax bills for any tax already paid by the trustees. There can be similar arrangements for non-resident landlords.

7.6.2. Capital Gains Tax

The above example of Bill and Ted is straightforward. But what if Ted says that his investment was only a loan to Bill, so that Bill could actually buy and own the house outright? Or, what if Ted is married, and says that his wife, Gertrude, should also be included for CGT purposes (and use her basic rate band/annual exemption) when the property is sold?

While legal ownership is relatively easy to determine, beneficial ownership can change relatively easily (or be more difficult to pin down in the first place). How the proceeds are divided by the parties is strongly indicative, of course, and HMRC's approach in such cases can be found in its Trusts and Estates manual (at TSEM9900 onwards). And also in the Capital Gains Manual CG70230.

7.6.3. Inheritance Tax

Many readers will be familiar with the 'gifts with reservation of benefit' IHT trap which, says that where a person gives away (for example) the family home, but retains the right to live in it, the home may be deemed never to have left that person's estate for IHT purposes.

This reflects that the original owner may have transferred legal ownership to another party, but has retained an equitable interest – a right to occupy the property – for himself.

7.6.4. Practical Tip

Legal ownership is more concerned with the responsibilities of land ownership, while beneficial ownership is about who benefits from or enjoys the use of the property. Quite rightly, tax usually follows the beneficial owner. But pinning down beneficial ownership can sometimes be problematic, particularly between co-owners and family members. It is worth keeping contemporaneous notes and documentation, in case they are needed later, such as in the event of an HMRC enquiry.

8. Offsetting Interest Charges From 6th April 2017

8.1. The New Rules

New rules were introduced, applying from April 2017, limiting relief for residential landlords for interest payments.

8.2. The Restrictions

The restrictions apply in respect of:

a) Income tax charged in relation to property businesses carried on by individuals (whether alone or in partnership), trustees and personal representatives of deceased estates and individuals who as beneficiaries of estates are chargeable to income tax. Companies carrying on property business are not affected.
b) Interest and other finance costs on loans taken out for a property business which involves the letting of residential properties. Loans which are wholly for commercial properties, or for properties which are used for a furnished holiday letting business are not affected.
c) Any incidental costs incurred in obtaining the loan. This includes items such as fees or commission payments.

8.3. Relevant Residential Property Lets

The restrictions apply to what the legislation terms a 'dwelling-related loan'. This means any amount borrowed for the purposes of a property business, to the extent to which both of the following apply:

- the business consists of receiving rental income from a dwelling-house, and
- the loan amount is used for that part of the business.

"Dwelling-house" has its normal dictionary meaning in this context, and can include part of a dwelling-house as well as the land and gardens attached to the house. However furnished holiday accommodation which is let commercially is specifically excluded from the definition of "dwelling-house".

A loan will be regarded as being for the purposes of a relevant property business if it is for the acquisition, construction or adaptation of the dwelling-house in question.

8.4. What A Property Business May Consist Of

A property business may consist of the letting of both a dwelling-house(s) and other lettings. Deductions for interest and finance costs will be restricted only in respect of any loan, or part of a loan, that is for the purpose of the dwelling-house part of the business. It is necessary to consider the purpose of the borrowing – the use made of the funds – during the period when the interest accrues.

Where the business has separate borrowings for the dwelling-house(s) letting and other letting parts of the business - for example where each property owned by the business has a specific mortgage for the acquisition of the property – then the interest on the mortgages for the residential properties will be subject to the restriction. Interest on the mortgages that relate to letting of other properties will not be restricted as long as the borrowings continue to be used for that purpose.

Where a property business consists of letting both a dwelling-house(s) and other letting then it may be necessary to apportion interest and finance costs on any loan which has been taken out for the purposes of the whole letting business. An example of this is a mortgage towards the purchase of a rental property which has a retail shop on the ground floor, with a separate residential flat on the first floor. The legislation does not stipulate how the apportionment is to be made, other than that it must be on a 'just and reasonable basis'.

8.5. Calculation of the restriction

The restriction to the amounts of 'dwelling-related loan" costs which may be deducted in arriving at taxable profit has been phased in over several years, beginning in 2017/18. The restriction applies as follows:

- 2017/18   75% of finance costs may be deducted from rental income
- 2018/19   50% of finance costs may be deducted from rental income
- 2019/20   25% of finance costs may be deducted from rental income
- Thereafter   0% of finance costs may be deducted from rental income

8.6. Calculation Of The Basic Rate Reducer

For individuals (including partners in a property rental partnership) the balance of finance costs which would otherwise qualify for relief but which because of the restriction has not been deducted in arriving at taxable rental profits, may be relieved at the basic rate of tax and deducted from tax liability for the tax year in question.

The landlord needs to look at three figures, and take the smallest of the three. a) Interest paid to the lender. b) Rental income. c) Adjusted total income (ATI). ATI is the individual's net income for the year from all sources, less savings income, and less allowances (e.g. personal allowance). Let's say an individual has employment income of £50,000, has rental income of £20,000, and pays £8,000 interest. From 2020/21 they are able to deduct £8,000 * 20% = **£1,600** from their final tax bill.

9. Offsetting Different Types Of Interest Charges

In this section you will learn about the different types of interest repayments that property investors may come across.

9.1. Interest On Mortgages

It is probably fair to say that this is the most common type of interest that is associated with property investors.

This interest relates to the amount you pay back to your mortgage lender that is above and beyond the initial amount that you borrowed.

> It does not matter if the mortgage is a 'repayment' or an 'interest only' mortgage. The fact that interest repayments have been made means that they can be offset.

This is illustrated through the following case study.

Interest on Mortgages

John buys an investment property for £100,000.

The finance for the property is made up from a £20,000 deposit (provided from his personal savings) and an £80,000 buy-to-let mortgage (provided by a High Street Bank).

In the tax year 2021-22 he pays £2,500 in mortgage interest.

So if he received £6,000 income from his property, he would be liable to pay tax on this £6,000. But he can knock £2,500 * 20% = £500 off his final tax bill.

9.2. A Note About 'Interest Only' And 'Repayment Mortgages'

As mentioned in the above tax tip, you are able to claim interest relief regardless of whether you have an 'interest only' mortgage or a 'repayment' mortgage.

9.2.1. Interest Only Mortgage

With an **interest only** mortgage you do actually only pay the interest that is charged on the amount that has been borrowed. The actual amount i.e. the capital amount remains the same and is usually due in one lump sum at the end of the mortgage term.

> **Interest Only Mortgage**
>
> Louise buys a property for £125,000 where her mortgage lender provides £100,000 on an interest only mortgage over 25 years.
>
> Her monthly interest repayment is £500.
>
> At the end of the mortgage term, she will still owe the £100,000 that has been borrowed.

9.2.2. Repayment Mortgage

With a **repayment** mortgage you pay both the interest and the capital amount on a monthly basis. However, you are only able to offset the amount that has been charged in interest. You cannot offset the capital repayments.

> **Repayment Mortgage**
>
> Same scenario as in the previous example. However, this time Louise goes for a repayment mortgage of £100,000.
>
> This means that her monthly repayments will be higher because she is repaying both the interest and part of the capital amount borrowed.
>
> She makes monthly repayments of £650, where £400 is the interest repayment and £250 is capital repayment.
>
> She is only able to claim tax relief for the interest part of the repayment i.e. the £400. She is not able to claim tax relief for the capital element of the repayment mortgage.

9.3. Interest On Personal Loans

> If you take out a personal loan that is used 'wholly and exclusively' for the purpose of the property, then the interest charged on this loan can also be offset.

The important point to note here is that personal loans *must* be used in connection with the property.

Following are some typical property investment scenarios detailing when the interest charged on a personal loan *can* be offset against the property income.

9.3.1. Loan Used For Providing Deposit

Most buy-to-let mortgage lenders require you to provide a 20% deposit before they will lend you the remaining 80% in the form of a mortgage.

If you don't have the 20% deposit, then it is likely that you may well need to finance the deposit by getting a personal loan.

If you do take out a personal loan for the 20% deposit, the interest charged on this loan can be offset against the property income.

If you are considering doing this, or have already done this, then what this means is that you have a 100% financed investment property, where interest charged on both the mortgage and the personal loan can be offset against the rental income.

Interest on Personal Loan Used For Deposit

Ali is desperate to buy his first investment property after seeing his pension fund plummet and his house value almost double within 5 years.

Unfortunately, (due to his lifestyle), he has no savings of his own but is in a job, earning £40,000 per annum.

He sees an investment property advertised for £100,000, but his mortgage lender requests a deposit of £15,000.

He sources this deposit by acquiring a personal loan at a rate of 9% per annum.

The bank then agrees to finance the remaining £85,000.

This means that Ali has a 100% financed investment property. Therefore, he is able to offset interest charged on both his loan and the BTL mortgage against his rental income.

9.3.2. Loan Used For Refurbishments/Developments

Periodically, you will need to refurbish or even develop a property.

Imagine that you have just purchased a property that needs totally re-decorating and modernising. If you take out a loan for this kind of work, then the interest charged on the loan can be offset against the property income.

Alternatively, you might decide to embark on a more expensive property extension, e.g., to build a conservatory.

Again, the same rule applies here: The interest charged on the loan can be offset.

> **Interest on Personal Loan Used for a Refurbishment**
>
> Karen buys an investment property for £100,000. She manages to pay the 15% deposit from her own personal savings and the remaining finance is acquired on a BTL mortgage.
>
> Before letting out the property she decides that a new bathroom suite will greatly increase the chances of the property getting let quickly. She prices a replacement bathroom suite at £2,000.
>
> Unfortunately, she has already stretched her personal savings account by funding the deposit for the property.
>
> Therefore, she applies for, and is successful, in obtaining a £2,000 personal loan at an interest rate of 10%.
>
> Because the personal loan is used to replace the bathroom suite in the investment property she is able to offset the interest charged on the loan against her rental income.

9.3.3. Loans Used For Purchasing Products

If you purchase goods from retailers where finance is available and these goods are used in your property, then the interest charged can also be offset.

This is more likely to happen if you are providing a fully furnished property, e.g., a luxury apartment.

If this is the case, then you may decide to buy the more expensive items on finance.

Such items are likely to include:

- sofas, dining table & chairs, beds;
- cooker, washing machine, fridge/freezer;
- carpets, flooring, etc.

If you are paying for these products over a period of time (e.g., 6, 12, or 18 months), then any interest charged by your creditor can be offset against your rental income.

> **Interest on Buy-Now-Pay-Later Loans**
>
> Continuing from the previous case study.
>
> Once the bathroom suite has been replaced she decides that the property should be offered fully furnished.
>
> She decides to buy some new kitchen furniture in a sale and buys it on a buy-now-pay later scheme where interest is charged at a rate of 27.9%.

> Again she is able to offset the interest charged on the loan against the rental income.

9.3.4. Loans To Continue The Running Of Your Business

There may be occasions when you need to borrow money because your need to pay some bills or employees but do not have sufficient funds in your account.

In such circumstances you may decide to apply for a short-term loan to make these payments. Again the interest charged on the loan can be offset against the property income.

> **Interest on Loan for Paying Bills & Employees**
>
> Alexander has a large portfolio of properties but has incurred a cash flow problem. This is because he has just paid for a major refurbishment on one of his properties by using funds in his property account, rather than acquiring some sort of finance.
>
> This decision means that he is unable to pay his employees (who work in his property business) their end of month salaries and some property related utility bills that are due.
>
> He applies for a short-term loan of £5,000 to make the necessary payments and interest is charged at 8%.
>
> His is able to offset the interest charged against the income from his properties because it is incurred for the purpose of his property business.

9.3.5. Interest On Overdrafts

If you have a separate bank account set-up for your property investment business then you may decide to apply for an overdraft rather than a personal loan.

If you decide to do this then as long as the overdraft is used for the purpose of the property business, then you can offset the interest charged on the overdraft.

> **Interest Charged on Overdrafts**
>
> Using the previous example. Instead of applying for a loan, Alexander decides to request a one-year overdraft limit on his account of £5,000. His application is successful and he is charged an interest rate of 7.5%.
>
> Whenever he uses his overdraft facility and interest is charged, he is able to offset it against his rental income.

9.4. Interest On Re-Mortgages

If you have a mortgage on your investment property, then it is highly likely that you will consider moving to another lender at some point.

The main reason for this is because you will be trying hard to find a better mortgage deal!

As interest rates have been changing over the past few years, more and more people have been re-mortgaging their investment properties to capitalise on the better deals and to help grow their property portfolios.

Below are some pointers about re-mortgaging.

a) If you re-mortgage your outstanding mortgage with another lender, then you can *still* offset the interest repayments.

> **Interest on Re-Mortgages**
>
> Timothy has an outstanding mortgage balance of £50,000 on his investment property. He decides to move his mortgage from the Nat West to Lloyds as they are offering a lower rate of interest.
>
> Timothy can still offset interest charged by Lloyds on the £50,000 re-mortgage.

b) If you re-mortgage for a lower amount, then you can still offset the whole mortgage interest.

> **Re-mortgaging for a Different Value**
>
> Imagine the same scenario as in the previous example, where Timothy has an outstanding balance of £50,000 on his investment mortgage.
>
> However, he inherits £20,000 from a family member, so he decides to use this toward lowering his mortgage liability.
>
> Therefore, he only re-mortgages to the value of £30,000 with Lloyds.
>
> Again, the interest charged on the £30,000 can be offset against the property income.

c) If you re-mortgage for a greater amount, then you can offset the additional interest in one of two circumstances:
   - if the additional amount borrowed is used for the purpose of an investment property, OR
   - even if is not used for the purpose of an investment property, but the total amount now borrowed is less than the value of the property when it started to be rented out. (Per Example 2 on BIM45700).

As property prices have sharply risen over the past few years, investors have been re-mortgaging their properties for higher values.

This is known as **releasing equity.**

If you have released equity or are considering doing this, then you need to follow the guidelines given above regarding the interest charged on personal loans.

You need to ask yourself,

'Is the additional equity release being used for the sole purpose of my property business?'

This can be illustrated through the following case study.

> **Releasing Equity**
>
> Timothy has an outstanding balance of £50,000 on his investment mortgage.
>
> However, his property value has appreciated considerably, so he decides to re-mortgage with Lloyds for £80,000.
>
> This means that he is releasing additional equity out of his current property to the value of £30,000.
>
> He decides to use the equity release in the following way:
>
> £20,000 is used to fund a new property investment, and it provides the deposit for his next buy-to-let investment. £10,000 is used to pay for a new car for his wife.
>
> Now, Timothy can *only* offset the interest charged on both the outstanding mortgage balance of £50,000 and the £20,000 he is using as a deposit for his next purchase.
>
> This is because this combined amount of £70,000 is used 'wholly and exclusively' for his property investments.
>
> However, he *cannot* use the interest charged on £10,000 for buying the car as this cost is not associated with his property investments.

d) Generally speaking, because it is possible to obtain a lower rate of interest on your residential mortgage, more and more investors are deciding to increase the borrowing on their main residence and using this to reduce the investment mortgages.

Releasing Equity from Main Residence

Jack and Louise have a residential mortgage on their private residence for £100,000. The interest rate is fixed at 4.5%. They also have a BTL investment property. The outstanding mortgage on this property is also £100,000 but the interest rate is at a higher rate of 6.5%.

Because their main residence has a value of £300,000, they release £100,000 equity from their main residence, at the same rate of 4.5%, and pay off the outstanding debt of £100,000 on the investment property.

Again the interest charged on the £100,000 equity release can be offset against the rental income off the investment property.

10. 'Wholly And Exclusively'

This section will address the term 'wholly and exclusively.'

If you have ever read and tried to digest the Property Income Manual, then you will have noticed that this phrase is consistently mentioned in the guide.

By the time you have finished this section, you will know how to test if an expense satisfies this rule and whether it can be offset against your property rental income.

10.1. Understanding The Term 'Wholly And Exclusively'

> HMRC state,
>
> **'You can't deduct expenses unless they are incurred wholly and exclusively for business purposes.'**

To put it simply, this statement means that if you incurred an expense that was not used for the purpose of your property, in any way at all, then you cannot offset the cost.

Whenever you incur a cost for your investment property, always ask yourself,

> **'Has the cost been incurred wholly and exclusively for the property?'**

If you can answer **YES** to this question, then it is highly likely you will be able to offset the cost against your property rental income.

10.2. What If Cost Is Not Wholly And Exclusively Incurred For Property?

Sometimes you may incur a cost that is not used 'wholly and exclusively' for your property. However, a portion of the cost has been incurred for your property.

For such situations HMRC provide the following guideline:

> **'Where a definite part or proportion of an expense is wholly and exclusively incurred for the purposes of the business, you can deduct that part or proportion.'**

What this effectively means is that you need to determine what part or proportion of the cost is attributed to your investment property. This is because you cannot offset the entire cost.

The following case study will help to illustrate this guideline.

Where Costs Are Not Wholly and Exclusively Incurred for Property

Bill has an investment property.

The bathroom is looking rather 'tired,' so he decides to re-tile it completely. He goes to a local tile shop, where they have an offer of 12 square metres of tiles for £240.

However, he only requires seven square metres for his investment property.

After some serious head scratching he appreciates that the deal is an excellent value for the money and too good to miss. He therefore purchases the tiles.

He decides to use the extra 5 square metres of tiles in his own house.

This means that the entire cost has not been incurred wholly and exclusively for the property. However, a portion of the cost, i.e., 7/12ths, has been incurred wholly and exclusively for the property.

He may therefore offset £140 (i.e., 7/12ths of £240) against his rental income.

10.3. Costs Of Maintenance And Repairs

> Once you have purchased and successfully let your property, any maintenance costs incurred that help prevent the property from deteriorating can be offset against your rental income.

It is very likely that at some point you will have to carry out some maintenance work to keep your property in an acceptable state of repair.

When this happens, you will be able to offset the cost against your property income as long as it satisfies the following condition.

- **It is not a capital improvement.**
  A capital improvement is when work is carried out that increases the value of the property.

Maintenance Cost

John is informed by his tenants that water is leaking from the upstairs bathroom into the downstairs living room.

He calls a plumber to repair the damaged bathroom water pipe and also hires a painter/decorator to redecorate the damaged ceiling.

The entire cost of the work is £300, and it can be offset against the rental income.

10.4. Typical Maintenance/Repair Costs

The following list details typical maintenance/repair costs that you are likely to incur and which you can offset against your rental income:

- repairing water/gas leaks, burst pipes, etc.;
- repairing electrical faults;
- fixing broken windows, doors, gutters, roof slates/tiles, etc.;
- repairing internal/external walls, roofs, floors, etc.;
- painting and redecorating the property;
- treating damp/rot;
- re-pointing, stone cleaning, etc.;
- hiring equipment to carry out necessary repair work;
- repairing existing fixtures and fittings which include:
    - radiators,
    - boilers,
    - water tanks,
    - bathroom suites,
    - electrical/gas appliances,
    - furniture, and furnishings, etc.

10.5. The Big Misconception About Costs When A Property Is First Let?

There is a common misconception among buy to let landlords – and some of their accountants – that the cost of repairs to a newly-purchased property cannot be claimed before it is first let out.

10.5.1. Allowable Expenses

In fact, such repairs are an allowable expense provided certain conditions are met.

The important distinction is between work on the property which is "capital expenditure" - effectively, part of the cost of acquiring the property and making it fit for use in the letting business, and expenditure which is no more than routine maintenance – even if that maintenance is quite extensive as a result of the previous owner's neglect.

10.5.2. The Test

The test is this: was the property fit to be let before the repairs were carried out? If it was, then the repairs are an allowable expense against the rent once the property is let.

The law on this subject is derived from two tax cases which were heard shortly after the end of the Second World War.

10.5.3. A Cinema

In one case, Odeon Cinemas claimed the cost of repairs to various cinemas they had bought up after the end of the war and refurbished before opening them to the public again.

Although the cinemas in question were in a poor state of repair, the Court was satisfied that they were nevertheless usable, and Odeon were simply carrying out routine maintenance which had been neglected during the war. They were also satisfied that the price Odeon paid for the cinemas was not significantly lower as a result of the condition they were in.

10.5.4. A Ship

The other case concerned a ship which was also bought just after the end of the war. It too was in a poor state of repair, to the extent that it was classified as not being seaworthy. Given the times, a temporary certificate of seaworthiness was granted on condition that the ship was sailed straight to a port where it could be extensively repaired.

When the claim for these repairs came to court, the verdict went against the ship-owners. This was because it was clear that (despite the temporary certificate granted because of the post-war shortage of ships) the ship was not fit for use and the repairs were necessary before it could be used for the owner's trade.

It was also the case that the price paid for the ship reflected the fact that it was unseaworthy. The cost of the repairs was therefore capital expenditure, being part of the cost of acquiring the ship as a useable asset for the trade, in contrast to the Odeon cinemas, which were already useable when purchased, and simply needed their neglected routine maintenance brought up to date.

10.5.5. Is Your Property A Cinema Or A Ship?

This distinction between capital expenditure and repairs applies to any work carried out on a property, at any stage in its ownership, and there is nothing special about work carried out before the first letting. The same rules apply, and expenditure on normal maintenance is an allowable expense whether the property has already been let or it has only just been purchased.

That is why a landlord should look at the property he has just bought for his letting business and consider whether it is more like a rather tatty cinema, or an unseaworthy ship!

If you have difficulty persuading your accountant that this is the correct view, tell him to go to HM Revenue and Customs' website, and look at PIM2030 in their Property Income Manual under "Repairs etc. after a property is acquired".

10.6. Capital Improvements

If you carry out a capital improvement, then you *cannot* offset this cost against your rental income.

This is because it is not classed as maintenance or repair work.

Capital Improvements

After years of owning his investment property, Fred applies for, and gets approval to add, a conservatory.

The cost of the conservatory is £20,000.

Because the conservatory has increased the value of the house by £30,000, it cannot be offset against the rental income.

Again, the cost will be offset against any capital gain that he makes when he sells the property.

REMEMBER: If you have made a capital improvement, then this cost can be claimed when you sell your property, so always keep your invoices.

11. Replacing Your Fixtures And Fittings

This section will help you to understand what is meant by the term **fixtures and fittings** and when you can offset the replacement of them against your income tax.

11.1. What Are Fixtures And Fittings?

These are items that are classed as being an integral part of the property. If a new tenant moves into a property, then they will expect these items to be in the property.

Examples of fixtures and fittings include:

- windows, doors, light fittings;
- kitchen units;
- bathroom suites;
- gas central heating systems and radiators or hot water supply tanks;
- gas fires, etc.

The most important point to understand about fixtures and fittings is that any cost incurred in repairing them or replacing them with a like-for-like product can be offset against the property rental income. This is regardless of whether the property is un-furnished, partly furnished, or fully furnished.

For the remainder of this section we will focus on the replacement of fixtures and fittings.

Two important conditions must be satisfied before you can offset the cost of replacing fixtures and fittings. These are the following.

   a) The cost must be a 'replacement' cost. In other words, it cannot be for the installation of fixtures and fittings that were not previously in the property.

   b) The cost must be for a similar, like-for-like product.

If both these conditions are met, then the cost can be deducted from the rental profits.

11.2. Replacing Fixtures And Fittings

Whenever you decide to replace existing fixtures and fittings, they are likely to fall into one of the following three categories:

   a) like-for-like replacement;
   b) like-for-like replacement but with capital improvements;
   c) replacement with superior fixtures and fittings.

Each of the above scenarios is treated differently when it comes to calculating your income tax bill, and each is illustrated in the following sections.

11.2.1. Like-For-Like Replacement

If you replace existing fixtures and fittings with similar like-for-like products, then the entire cost can be offset against the income tax bill.

> **Replacing With Like-for-Like (1)**
>
> Alex has been renting out his buy-to-let property for seven years and decides that it is now time to change the bathroom suite.
>
> He finds a similar bathroom suite of comparable quality that costs £500. The cost of having the old suite removed and the new one fitted is also £500.
>
> This means that the entire project costs £1,000.
>
> This whole amount can be offset against the annual rental income.

11.2.2. What If It Is Not Possible To Replace With Like-For-Like?

HMRC appreciate that it is not possible to replace with a like-for-like product in all instances. This is especially true if you are replacing something that is several years old as a like-for-like product may no longer be available.

In such circumstances, it is possible to replace with a superior item, especially if it is of a similar cost.

> **Replacing With Like-for-Like (2)**
>
> Alex also decides to replace the wooden, single-glazed windows as they are starting to rot. The windows are more than 10 years old.
>
> The cost of replacing with similar single-glazed windows is £3,500, and this includes the fitting and removal of the old, rotten windows.
>
> However, the cost of replacing the windows with UPVC double-glazed windows is cheaper and costs £3,400. This price also includes the fitting and removal of the old windows.
>
> Although the UPVC double-glazed windows are of a superior quality, HMRC accept that these types of windows are the 'standard' in all new build properties.
>
> Therefore, it is possible to use these as replacements and offset the entire cost incurred.

11.2.3. Like-For-Like Replacement But With Capital Improvements

If you replace the existing fixtures and fittings with a like-for-like product but also make a capital improvement, then you can only offset the cost of the like-for-like replacement.

> **Replacing With Like-for-Like but with Capital Improvement**
>
> Alex also decides to replace the kitchen units.
>
> The cost of replacing the kitchen units with like-for-like replacements is £1,600. However, he has some additional space that he wishes to utilise, so he orders an additional three units at a cost of £600.
>
> Alex is able to offset the cost of the £1,600 like-for-like replacement against his rental income.
>
> However, the additional three units are treated as a capital improvement, and this cost cannot be offset against the rental income.
>
> Instead, the cost of the additional units can be offset against any capital gain arising when the property is sold.

11.2.4. Replacement With Superior Fixture And Fittings

If you replace the existing fixtures and fittings with superior fixture and fittings, then it will be treated as a capital improvement.

12. Other Ways To Reduce Your Income Tax Bill

In the strategies to date you have learned about the common costs that can be offset against the rental income.

In this section you will now become familiar with numerous other typical costs that a property investor is likely to incur and that can be offset against the rental income.

12.1. Rents, Rates, And Insurance

The following costs are incurred by property investors when the property is let or when the property is empty and between lets.

12.1.1. Rents

The most common type of rent that an investor is likely to incur is ground rent. Landlords are liable to pay this rent on any leasehold property/land, and therefore any such expenditure can be offset against the rental income.

12.1.2. Rates

If you decide to pay any of the following rates on your property, then they can be offset against the rental income:

- water;
- electricity;
- gas;
- council tax;
- service charges;
- TV licence;
- telephone line rental;
- satellite TV charges, etc.

12.1.3. Insurance

Any insurance premiums that you pay for your properties or products/services relating to your property can also be offset against the rental income.

The most common premiums you are likely to pay will include the following:

- building insurance;
- contents insurance;
- insurance cover for service supplies such as
  - gas central heating,
  - plumbing insurance,
  - electrical insurance;
- insurance cover for appliances such as
  - washer/dryer,
  - fridge/freezer,
  - television, etc.

12.2. Can I Offset Pre-Trading Expenditure?

This is a bit of a grey area as far as taxation goes.

The rules for pre-trading expenditure are quite complex, but in theory you can claim expenses incurred in the seven years before commencement of the rental 'business.

The expenses are treated as incurred on the first day the rental 'business' starts.

Having said that, HMRC will want to examine these expenses closely with a view to establishing whether they were incurred 'wholly and exclusively' for the purposes of the 'trade.'

Again in theory HMRC can disallow any expense which has a duality of purpose, but in practice they will usually allow a split to be made.

They will also examine the expenses to see whether they are capital or revenue in nature.

Below is a list of some common types of pre-trading expenditure you are likely to incur before you buy your property:

- travel costs
- the cost of purchasing dedicated trade/magazines for helping you to find your property;
- the cost of telephone calls when phoning estate agents/property vendors, etc.

The important point to note is that each occurrence of a pre-trading expenditure must be incurred wholly and exclusively for the property.

12.3. Carrying Over Rental Losses

> Any rental losses made on a property can be carried forward into the next financial year.

Sometimes you will incur a rental loss on your property investment. Rental losses can be incurred intentionally or unintentionally. The important point to note is that any losses can be carried forward into the next year and can be used to reduce your tax liability for that year.

Carrying Over Rental Losses

After three years of owning his two-bedroom buy-to-let property, John decides to replace the bathroom suite. The cost of replacing it with a like-for-like replacement is £2,500.

His rental income for the property is £4,800 annually, but after all his annual expenses are deducted, including the cost of the replacement bathroom suite, etc., he is left with a £1,000 rental loss.

> This loss can be carried forward and offset against his rental income the following year.

12.4. Claiming Travel Costs

Below is an explanation of travel costs by Jennifer Adams.

A rented property portfolio may not be placed in the same street or even the same town as your main residence or place of work. Travel from one property to another, as the landlord dealing with problems as they arise, does cost. That cost is allowed as an expense against rental income received.

The treatment of travel expenses is similar to that as incurred by a trade or profession, such that to be allowed two key conditions need to be met:

- The expense must be related to the property in that it satisfies the '*wholly and exclusively*' test; and

- It must not be incurred as a capital improvement such that the value of the property is increased.

12.4.1. 'Wholly And Exclusively'

Confirmation that profits of a property are calculated using the same rules as for the computation of trading income is to be found in the tax legislation at s 272 of the *Income Tax (Trading and Other Income Act) 2005* (ITTOIA 2005) and hence the '*wholly and exclusively*' rule applies such that there must not be duality of purpose of the expense incurred.

12.4.2. Office Based At Home

It is a question of fact as to whether the landlord carries on the rental business from his home. If so, the cost of all trips from home (e.g. to check on the investment property/liaise with tenants etc.) are fully allowable, provided that the visit is not also combined with a personal reason.

However, a deduction would still be possible for a journey where any personal benefit is incidental (i.e. '*de minimis*'); for example, the trip is made to the rental property, but the landlord stops on the way to pick up a newspaper.

Furthermore, when making a claim for travelling expenses between the home base and a let property the real reason for the trip may need to be considered carefully.

For example, a landlord lets his main residence in Woking whilst working away from home in Brighton. He has travelled to Woking with his family to visit relatives at Christmas. Whilst in the area he may decide to drop by the rented property for a visit - this will be deemed a 'duality of purpose' visit, not fulfilling the 'wholly and exclusively' rules and hence the cost of travel will be disallowed for tax purposes.

Similarly, if the owner lives in London and has both a holiday home and a letting property based a few miles away from each other in Dorset, the cost of travel would only be allowed if the trip was made straight from the London base to the letting property without stopping at the holiday home first.

However, it would be fair to claim mileage from the holiday home to the let property.

12.4.3. Office Outside Of Home

If the property business is *managed* from an office outside of the home then HMRC deems the business not to be carried on at home, even if the property owner sometimes works from home. In this situation the cost of journeys between home and either the property let or that office base will not be allowable.

However, the cost of travel from the office to and from the properties, and also between properties, will be allowable provided that the trip is incurred '***wholly and exclusively***' for rental business purposes.

12.4.4. Use Of A Letting Agent

Some landlords engage a letting agent to manage the collection of rents, organise services etc. Where such an agent carries out all (or virtually all) the duties relating to the letting activity, it is likely that the rental business is being conducted through the agent.

In such circumstances, the business 'base' is deemed to be the agent's office and as such travelling expenses from the landlords' home to the property are not allowable but will be from the agents office to the property.

12.4.5. Relevant Tax Cases

Under the tax legislation (ITTOIA 2005, s 272) these cases are now relevant to a rental business:

- **Newsom v Robertson [1952]** - a barrister frequently worked from home but his chambers were separate. As such he was deemed not to be carrying on his profession from home and travel between home and chambers was not ***wholly and exclusively*** incurred for the purposes of his profession.

- **Horton v Young [1971]** - it was found that the claimant did carry on his trade from home and as such travel from home to the various sites at which he worked was undertaken for the purposes of the trade and claimable.

12.4.6. How Much To Claim?

- **Capital expenditure**

If the landlord uses his own car for travel, the full capital purchase cost of the car is not allowable; rather a proportion is, as capital allowances, claimed in the proportion of business use.

The '***wholly and exclusively***' rule also applies to that amount claimed and as with car running expenses only the business proportion is allowed. For detailed guidance see https://www.gov.uk/hmrc-internal-manuals/property-income-manual/pim2010 and PIM2220.

- **Running expenses**

There are two methods of calculation for car expenses incurred - the same as for other business expenses.

1. A fixed rate for each mile travelled on business using HMRC's fixed mileage rates. Currently the first 10,000 business miles in relation to the rental business are claimed at 45p and 25p thereafter. This method of calculation is only available where certain conditions are met.

2. On an actual basis, such that the actual expenses (fuel, repairs, insurance etc.) are totalled and apportioned between business and private percentage using detailed records. For example, if a landlord agrees with HMRC that 70% of mileage incurred relates to expenses for the property business a 70% deduction is claimed (the same percentage is used for the capital allowance claim). Provided that the landlord proposes a percentage to add back/disallow which reasonably reflects the private element, HMRC will usually accept.

12.4.7. Misc. Travel Costs

If the trip to visit the property requires an overnight stay, then hotel costs and meals in restaurants can be claimed; if public transport is used then the claim is the cost of the ticket.

12.4.8. Foreign Travel

- If a foreign property is rented out then similar to any other business travel costs, car parking, hotel expenses, petrol, toll charges, flight costs etc. can be claimed providing that you can prove no 'duality of purpose' (e.g. that you did not visit the property whilst also on holiday)
- Incidentally, all foreign property rentals are treated as one business. Hence a claim can be made for the cost of travel to Dubai to look for a possible new rental property against the rental income from a villa already owned in Spain.

12.4.9. Expenses When Not Available For Letting

Expenses incurred during any period whilst the property is *'not available for letting'*, are not deductible for tax purposes. This not only means that travel costs cannot be claimed but it also results in restrictions being made on other expenses that would otherwise be claimed including the mortgage interest.

12.5. General Property Costs

If you have a portfolio and incur expenses then it may not be possible to attribute the cost to a single property. This is because the expenditure may have been for all of the properties.

A good example of this is when purchasing decorating materials for a property. In such circumstances you can either:

- apportion the cost against the properties, or
- have a separate listing of generic expenses to add on at the end when you combine all the incomes and expenditures.

Either way is fine, as it makes no difference to the tax position, though practically the latter option may be easier and simpler to implement.

12.6. Storage Costs

A cost incurred by an increasing number of investors is storage costs.

The cost of renting storage space is allowable against rental income. The reason is that it fulfils the principal criteria of "wholly and exclusively", as the cost was incurred for the purpose of your property business. If you never had rented property then you would not be incurring such costs.

Storage Costs

John owns 5 properties which are all fully furnished. However, he finds a new long-term tenant for his property who has his own furniture and furnishings. John decides that he will empty the property and store the furniture in rented storage. The cost of rental storage is £450. This amount can be offset against the rental income as it has been incurred 'wholly and exclusively' for the purpose of the rental business.

12.7. Other Common Landlord Expenditures

Below is a list of other common costs that a landlord will incur that can be offset against the rental income:

- safety certificates, e.g., gas and electrical safety;
- stationery, e.g., stamps, envelopes, books;
- computer equipment;
- bad debts;
- legal and professional costs, e.g., accountancy costs;
- service costs, e.g., window cleaner, gardener;
- furniture/appliance rentals;
- advertisement costs;
- letting agent costs;
- books, magazines, etc.;
- security/smoke alarms;
- telephone calls, including mobile telephone bills (but make sure you have an itemised bill to prove the calls made);
- bank charges (e.g., interest charged on property bank account).

12.8. Can I Offset The Cost Of A Property Seminar?

During the property investment boom a large number of potential and inexperienced investors attended seminars and paid thousands of pounds for learning about various property investment techniques.

A common question that arises is whether the cost of the seminar can be offset against any future income tax bill.

When asked the question **'Can I offset the cost of a £5,000 property seminar?'** Arthur Weller provides the following guidance:

If the cost of the seminar is wholly and exclusively for the purposes of the trade presently carried out by the taxpayer, then it is allowable.

Here is what HMRC have to say about the matter:

> *'Expenditure on training courses attended by the proprietor of a business with the purpose of updating his or her skills and professional expertise is normally revenue expenditure, which is deductible from profits of the business provided it is incurred wholly and exclusively for the purposes of the trade or profession carried on by the individual at the time the training is undertaken'.*

So what exactly does that mean?

Already a property investor
If you are already a property investor, with a portfolio, and attend the course to update your investment skills, then you can offset the entire cost.

You can offset the cost as you will be regarded as updating your skills.

When You CAN Offset the Cost of a £5,000 Property Course

Bill has been investing in property since 2010 and has built a portfolio of 12 properties.

However, in 2021 he decides take property investment more seriously and attends a £5,000 course to update and sharpen his investment skills so that he can focus on emerging areas for investment.

The entire cost of the course can be offset against his rental income.

New to property investment
However, if you want to start investing in property and attend a course to learn how to do this, then you will not be able to offset the costs against the rental income.

You cannot offset the cost as you will not be 'updating' your skills in your current profession.

> **When You CANNOT Offset the Cost of a £5,000 Property Course**
>
> Following the corona pandemic, John decides that the only way he will be able to maintain his lifestyle when he retires is if he invests in property.
>
> So, in 2021 he attends a property investment course to learn all about property investment. Shortly after the course he buys his first investment property. The cost of the course cannot be offset against any future rental income.

<u>A word of warning</u>
If you do decide to make a claim, it could well trigger an investigation. HMRC do keep a close eye on large amounts being claimed, so be warned!

HMRC have now slightly relaxed their position and are prepared to allow expenditure on courses which are ancillary to the owner's main trade. See examples on BIM35660.

12.9. Capital Allowances For Landlords

If you decide to purchase a piece of equipment or an asset that is used for the purpose of the business, then you can claim an 18% annual depreciation allowance. Examples of such assets include:

- Computers and office furniture (that you use in your own home for running the business)
- Tools for maintaining upkeep of properties i.e. DIY tools
- Vehicles (please note that there are new rules for claiming capital allowances on vehicles for expenditure incurred from April 09 onwards).

The depreciation allowance can be claimed annually until the equipment/asset is disposed of. Here is an example that shows how the 18% depreciation allowance works.

> **Capital Allowances for Assets**
>
> Wasim has a portfolio of five investment properties. He also carries out much of the maintenance and repairs on the properties himself, so he decides to purchase professional DIY toolkit for £150 in April 2012. The annual depreciation allowance is calculated as follows:
>
> | Tax Year | Toolkit Value | Annual Rate | Annual Allowance |
> |---|---|---|---|
> | 2015-2016 | £150 | 18% | £27 |
> | 2016-2017 | £123 | 18% | £22 |
> | 2017-2018 | £101 | 18% | £18 |
> | 2018-2019 | £83 | 18% | £15 |
> | 2019-2020 | £68 | 18% | £12 |

> As you can see from the above example, the amount that can be claimed on an annual basis continues to decrease as the toolkit value decreases.

A landlord can claim Annual Investment Allowance on his expenditure. See CA23080 for the rules.

13. Running Your Property Business From Home

Many small businesses are run from home and a proportion of the costs of running and maintaining the home can be deducted in computing the profits of the business.

Broadly speaking, expenses fall into two categories – fixed costs and running costs. Fixed costs are those that have to be incurred regardless of the level of trade. Costs that relate to the house as a whole will generally fall into this category. Running costs (or variable costs) are costs that vary depending on the extent of use, such as electricity.

This strategy looks at how relief may be obtained for the fixed cost and at example of typical fixed costs in respect of which relief may be available.

13.1. Nature Of Relief

Where a business is run from home and part of the home is set aside solely for business use for a specific period, a proportion of the fixed costs incurred in relation to the home will be allowed as a deduction in computing the business profits. It will generally be necessary to apportion the fixed costs between the business and non-business element. A reasonable basis of apportionment would be one which reflects the proportion of the house used for solely business purposes and the time for which it is so used.

Using an area of the house solely for business purposes can have capital gains tax consequences, as the main residence exemption does not apply to any part of the property used for business use. Where only a small part of the house is used solely for business, in most cases the availability of the annual exemption means this is rarely a problem in practice, as any chargeable gain arising is normally covered by the annual exemption. However, to be on the safe side it is sensible to set aside the room used for the business for sole business use during working hours to preserve the deduction for fixed costs but to make it available to the family in evenings and at weekends to keep it within the main residence exemption.

13.2. Typical Fixed Costs

Costs which may be incurred in relation to a house or other property and which are classified as fixed costs include:

- buildings and contents insurance;
- council tax;
- mortgage interest;
- rent; and
- repairs and maintenance.

Each of these is discussed in more detail below.

13.3. Insurance

Depending on the nature of the policy, insurance can be either a fixed or a variable cost. Buildings insurance will generally cover the whole property, and where a business is operated from home a deduction can be obtained for a proportion of the premium.

As regards contents insurance, if contents are covered as part of a general buildings and contents policy, a proportion of the total premium can be deducted; likewise, in relation to a separate contents policy that covers all household contents and does not exclude business items. However, if there is a specific trade policy, the premiums for that will be deductible in full, but there will be no deduction in relation to the domestic policy.

13.4. Council Tax

The extent to which a deduction is permitted in respect of council tax will depend on the circumstances. Council tax is a property-based tax payable on chargeable dwellings. By contrast, business rates are charged on commercial property. Depending on the size and scale of the business and the degree to which the premises are used for business purposes, the council may charge business rates.

However, where a trader merely sets aside a room in his or her home as an office, it is likely that only a council tax charge will apply. Where this is the case, the trader can claim a proportion of the council tax as a deduction in computing the profits of his or her business.

13.5. Mortgage Costs

Where the house is subject to a mortgage, a deduction may be permissible in respect of a portion of the mortgage costs. However, where the mortgage is a repayment mortgage it is necessary to split the payments into the capital repayment element and the interest element. Repayments of capital are not deductible, whereas a deduction is allowed in respect of the interest element and the trader can claim a portion of the interest element of a mortgage as a deduction in computing profits.

13.6. Rent

Where the trader rents his or her home and runs a business from a home office, a deduction is also available in computing profit if part of the home is used solely for business purposes. The allowable amount is the proportion of the rent payable to the landlord that is attributable to that part of the home used solely for business purposes.

It should be noted that where the business is run as a limited company, the homeowner can charge rent to his or her company in respect of the part of the home used by the company. The rent paid is deductible by the company in computing the profits for corporation tax purposes, and the homeowner is taxed on the rent that he or she receives. By contrast, where the business is operated by a sole trader, the homeowner cannot charge the business rent.

13.7. Repairs And Maintenance

All buildings will need some general maintenance at some point. Where part of the home is used solely for business purposes, a deduction is permitted for a proportion of general household repairs and maintenance to the extent that they apply to the property generally, rather than to a specific room.

Examples of repairs and maintenance costs which may be apportioned include roof repairs and painting the exterior of a property. However, where the repairs or maintenance relate solely to a part of the room, which is not used for business purposes, no deduction is permitted. By contrast, repairs or maintenance that relate wholly to the part that is used for business purposes are deductible in full.

It should be noted that no relief is available in respect of capital expenditure and a distinction is drawn between a repair (for which a deduction may be allowed) and improvements which are capital in nature and not deductible in computing profits. As a general rule, a repair restores something to its original condition, whereas an improvement significantly enhances it.

13.7.1. Practical Tip

It is easy to overlook the fixed costs of running a home when computing business profits, but it can be worthwhile claiming a deduction where part of the home is used exclusively for business. An additional deduction is available for running costs, which can be claimed either by reference to the actual costs incurred or by using the statutory simplified expenses deduction.

14. Tenant Deposits: Traps & Tips

14.1. Deposits From Tenants

It is common practice for a landlord to take a deposit from a tenant when letting a property to cover the cost of any damage caused to the property by the tenant. A deposit of this nature may be referred to as a security deposit, a damage deposit or a rental deposit. The landlord may also ask for a holding deposit in return for taking the property off the market while the necessary paperwork is undertaken.

14.2. Security Deposits

It is normal practice for landlords to take a security deposit from tenants when letting residential property. The purpose of the deposit is to cover items such as damage to the property that extends beyond normal wear and tear, the cost of having the property, including the carpets, professionally cleaned, removing any rubbish from the property, unpaid rent and such like. The items covered by the security deposit should be stated in the letting agreement.

The deposit charged can be up to two months' rent, although in practice six weeks' rent is common.

Deposits taken by a landlord or agent for an assured shorthold tenancy in England or Wales are protected by Government authorised schemes. There are three possible schemes:

- the Deposit Protection Service scheme;
- the Tenancy Deposits Solution scheme; and
- The Dispute Service scheme.

To remove the need to go to court to settle disputes over retention and repayment of the deposit, each scheme features an alternative dispute resolution service. In the event that there is a dispute regarding the repayment of the deposit in the case of damage or unpaid rent, the alternative dispute resolution service will arbitrate.

The burden of proof falls on the landlord or agent, who will need to provide evidence to support their claim that all or part of the deposit should be retained. If there is no dispute, the tenant's deposit should be returned to the tenant at the end of the tenancy.

The extent to which the deposit is included as income of the rental business depends on whether all or part of the deposit is retained by the landlord. In a straightforward case where a security deposit is taken by the landlord, held for the period of the tenancy and returned to the tenant at the end of the rental period, the deposit is not included as income of the property rental business.

However, if at the end of the tenancy agreement the landlord retains all or part of the deposit to cover damage to the property, cleaning costs or other similar expenses, the amount retained is included as income of the property rental business.

The retained deposit is a receipt of the business in the same way as rent received from the tenant. However, the actual costs incurred by the landlord in making good the damage or having the property professionally cleaned are deducted in computing the profits of the business.

The retained deposit is reflected as rental income of the property rental business for the period in which the decision to retain the deposit is taken, rather than for the period in which the deposit was initially collected from the tenant.

Example

Bill purchases a property as a buy to let investment. He lets the property out in September 2019. He collects a security deposit of £1,000 from the tenant. The terms of the deposit are set out in the tenancy agreement.

The let comes to an end in September 2021. When checking out the tenant, it transpires that the tenant has failed to have the carpets professionally cleaned, as per the terms of the agreement, and also that he has damaged a door, which needs to be repaired.

After discussion, Bill and the tenant agree that Bill will retain £250 of the deposit to cover cleaning and repair costs. The balance of the deposit (£750) is returned to the tenant in October 2021.

Bill spends £180 having the carpets professionally cleaned and £75 having the door repaired.

Bill prepares accounts for the property rental business to 31 March each year.

When preparing accounts for the year to 31 March 2022, Bill must include as income the £250 retained from the tenant. However, he can deduct the actual cost of cleaning the property (£180) and repairing the door (£75). As the amount actually spent (£255) exceeds the amount retained, he is given relief for the additional £5 in computing the profits of his property rental business.

The balance of the deposit returned to the tenant is not taken into account as income of the business.

As stated in the article on use of the property rental toolkit in our September issue, HMRC recognise that accounting for deposits can sometimes cause problems. Guidance on income that should be taken into account in computing the profits of a property rental business can be found in their Property Income Manual at PIM1052 (see https://www.gov.uk/hmrc-internal-manuals/property-income-manual/pim1052).

14.3. Holding Deposit

Holding deposits are another form of deposit commonly taken by landlords, particularly in periods where the letting market is buoyant and demand for property is high. As the name suggests, a holding deposit is paid by the tenant to secure the property while the tenancy agreement is signed. In return, the landlord will take the property off the market.

A holding deposit is usually in the region of one week's rent. The terms governing the use of the deposit and the circumstances in which it may be retained by the landlord should be set out in a holding deposit agreement so all parties know where they stand.

In the event that the let falls through and under the terms of the agreement the landlord retains some or all of the deposit as compensation for the inconvenience and costs incurred in relation to the prospective let, the amount of the retained deposit should be included as income of the property rental business. However, the landlord would be able to claim a deduction for any costs actually incurred in relation to aborted let, such as advertising or legal fees.

In the event that the let goes ahead, the holding deposit would either be returned to the tenant or used to form part of the security deposit (see above). If the holding deposit is returned, it does not form part of the income of the business. Where the holding deposit is used as part of the security deposit, as explained above, it is only taken into account to the extent that it is retained by the landlord to cover damage etc. at the end of the let.

14.3.1. Practical Tip

As a general rule, deposits taken from tenants only form part of the income of the property rental business to the extent that the deposit is ultimately retained by the landlord. Any deposits that are merely held on the tenant's behalf before being returned to the tenant are not taken into account as income. On the other side of the coin, a deduction is given for any costs actually incurred by the landlord in making good damage etc. covered under the terms of the deposit agreement.

14.4. Tax Treatment Of 'Gifted Deposits'?

A recent case before the First-tier Tribunal (Day and Anor v Revenue & Customs [2015] UKFTT 142 (TC)) holds some valuable lessons for landlords selling a buy-to-let property.

One of the properties in the above case had been sold using a 'gifted deposit' scheme.

14.4.1. Gifted Deposit Schemes

These schemes used to be very popular and were promoted as a way of becoming a property owner without having to come up with any of the purchase price. The seller of the property would agree to take (say) 5% less than the asking price (which was itself often a somewhat inflated one), but this would be done by the seller making a 'gift' to the buyer of the 5% difference. The buyer could then obtain a 95% mortgage on the stated purchase price, but the other 5% was provided by the seller so the buyer had none of their own money invested in the property.

Everyone seemed quite relaxed about this practice, even though to me it looked very much like a fraud on the lender of the money if they were not informed about the 'gift'. I recall raising this with a senior manager at one of the high street banks and asking what he thought about it. He asked me one question: 'In this hypothetical situation, does the buyer keep up with the mortgage payments?' When I replied 'yes', he gave me his professional opinion: 'Why should I care, then?'

This particular scheme was operated in the above case with the full knowledge of the lender involved – indeed the scheme was organised by the Halifax. Under the scheme, Mr Day and his co-investor effectively paid the 5% deposit on the sale to themselves, purportedly on behalf of the buyers, and the Halifax provided the buyers with a loan of the other 95% of the sale price. The point was to enable the Halifax to lend the buyers the whole of the actual purchase price whilst being able to record it as a 95% mortgage rather than a 100% one.

14.4.2. Tax Treatment

HMRC contended that the sale proceeds for capital gains tax (CGT) purposes should be the whole amount shown in the sale documentation (£66,300), rather than the price after the 'gifted deposit' of £62,985.

The Tribunal described the £66,300 as 'a label' and agreed that the correct sale proceeds were the amount after the gifted deposit - £62,985.

The important point, however, was what they said about gifted deposits in general and their view of the rights and wrongs of them. In the Day case, the gifted deposit had been paid with the full knowledge (indeed, with the encouragement) of the Halifax, the lender concerned. The Tribunal suggested their view might have been very different if the deposit had been 'gifted' without the lender's knowledge (as many were when this was a popular ruse in the buy-to-let market).

They did not mince their words, either:

"If the appellants had fraudulently paid the deposit in order to help the purchasers obtain a 95% mortgage, we might well not have been persuaded that the appellants could rely on that fraud to reduce their tax liability."

The thing that saved Mr Day and his co-investor was that this was one of the 'respectable' gifted deposits, because the lender concerned knew about it and indeed was promoting it. Things might have been very different if it had been one of the 'under the counter' schemes that were around at the time.

14.4.3. Practical Tip

If you bought a property using a gifted deposit scheme, the correct purchase price for CGT purposes when you come to sell it is likely to be the price net of the gifted deposit.

If anyone suggests using a gifted deposit, make certain the lender is fully aware of what is going on, and agrees to it.

15. Cash Basis For Landlords

15.1. Introduction

The cash basis is the default basis to be used by eligible unincorporated property businesses in working out the taxable profit of loss for their property income business.

An unincorporated landlord must use the cash basis if they are eligible to use it, unless they elect for the cash basis not to apply. Landlords who are excluded from the cash basis or elect for it not to apply must instead prepare accounts in accordance with Generally Accepted Accounting Principles (GAAP) under the accruals basis.

The cash basis only applies to unincorporated property businesses – property companies must use the accruals basis.

The cash basis can be used for furnished holiday lettings, and where rent-a-room relief is claimed where the rental receipts exceed the rent-a-room limit. The special tax regime for furnished holiday lettings is to be abolished from 6 April 2025.

15.2. Cash Basis Vs Accruals Basis

The two methods that may be used to calculate the taxable profits or losses of a property income business are the cash basis and the accruals basis. Landlords that are not eligible to use the cash basis must use the accruals basis. The cash basis is the default basis and where the landlord meets the eligibility criteria but wants to use the accruals basis, they must elect for this basis to apply.

15.2.1. Nature of the Cash Basis

The cash basis is the simpler of the two methods. It only takes account of money in and money out. Income is recognised when the cash is received and expenses are recognised when the bill is paid. There are no debtors or prepayments or any creditors or accruals to worry about. From this perspective, it makes the accounting very easy.

> **Nature of the Cash Basis**
>
> Ali is a landlord and prepares his accounts on the cash basis for each tax year. He receives rent of £1,500 for April 2024 on 1 April 2024. A plumber repairs a leak in the property on 31 March 2024. Ali pays the plumber's bill on 7 April 2024.
>
> Under the cash basis, the rent of £1,500 received on 1 April 2024 is taken into account in working out Ali's profits for 2023/24 as the money was received in that year. It does not matter that most of it relates to the period from 6/4/24 to 30/4/24 which falls in the 2024/25 tax year.
>
> Likewise, Ali receives relief for the plumbing bill in 20242/5 as the bill was paid in the 2024/25 tax year. It does not matter that the work was undertaken in 2023/24.

15.2.2. Nature of the Accruals Basis

Under the accruals basis, income and expenditure are taken into account in the period to which they relate, rather than the period in which income is received or expenses are paid.

Consequently, it is more complicated, as there may be debtors and creditors to take into account, and prepayments and accruals to work out. Thus in the above example, £250 of the rent of £1,500 received on 1 April 2024 which relates to the period from 1 to 5 April 2024 would be taken into account in 2023/24 and the remaining £1,250, which relates to the remainder of April 2024, would be taken into account in 2024/25. Relief for the plumbing bill would be given in 2023/24 as the work was undertaken in that year.

15.3. Cash Basis Eligibility

The cash basis applies unless the landlord ticks one of the boxes which prohibit its use.

The cash basis cannot be used in a tax year in which at least one of the following applies. Instead, profits or losses must be computed in accordance with GAAP under the accruals basis.

- A – The property business is run by company, a limited liability partnership, trustees or a partnership with at least one non-individual member.

- B – Receipts that are brought into account under the cash basis are more than £150,000 (proportionately reduced if the business is carried on for less than one year).

- C – The property business is carried on with a spouse or civil partner who uses the accruals basis.

- D -- Business premises renovation allowance has been claimed and this gives rise to a balancing adjustment in the tax year.

- E -- An election has been made for accounts to be prepared under UK GAAP.

Thus, the cash basis will apply to an unincorporated property business for a tax year if receipts (computed on the cash basis) are £150,000 or less and neither C nor D applies and the landlord has not elected to use the accrual basis.

Where a property business is run jointly with a spouse or civil partner, both must use the same basis of preparation. Therefore, a landlord cannot use the cash basis if their spouse or civil partner must use the accrual basis (for example, because they have cash basis receipts in excess of £150,000).

15.4. Election Not To Use The Cash Basis

If the landlord is eligible to use the cash basis but would prefer to use the accruals basis, for example to get earlier relief for expenses, he must elect to do so, This must be done within one year of the tax return filing date for the year for which the election is to apply (i.e. by 31 January 2026 for 2023/24 and by 31 January 2027 for 2024/25).

15.5. Relief For Revenue Expenses

Under the cash basis, as for the accruals basis, relief is given for revenue expenses to the extent that they are wholly and exclusively incurred for the purposes of the property business.

However, under the cash basis relief is given at the time at which the expense is paid, not for the period to which it relates.

For unincorporated residential landlords relief for interest and other finance costs is given as a tax reduction for 20% of the finance costs, rather than as a deduction in computing profits. Landlords with furnished holiday lets and non-residential lets can deduct interest and finance costs in full when computing taxable profits. However, it should be noted that the furnished holiday letting regime is to come to an end on 5 April 2025. For 2025/26 and subsequent years, profits from furnished holiday lettings will be taxed in the same way, and form part of the same property rental business, as other residential lets under the same ownership and relief for interest and finance costs will be given as a 20% tax reduction rather than as a deduction in computing profits.

Landlords using the cash basis can take advantage of the simplified expenses system to calculate a deduction for vehicle expenses using mileage rates rather than actual costs, unless capital allowances have been claimed for the car.

15.6. Relief For Capital Expenditure

Special rules apply to provide relief for capital expenditure under the cash basis. The rules allow capital expenditure to be deducted when working out profits unless the expenditure is of a type for which such a deduction is prohibited. The main categories of capital expenditure which cannot be deducted in working out profits are expenditure incurred in connection with the provision, alteration or disposal of land and expenditure on cars. However, the cost of a van can be deducted. The prohibition on the deduction of expenditure in connection with the provision, alteration of disposal of land also covers expenditure on a building, wall, ceiling, door, gate, shutter, window, stair, waste disposal system, sewerage or drainage system or a shaft or other structure in which a lift, hoist, escalator or moving walkway may be installed. However, expenditure on other assets which are installed or otherwise fixed to the land so as to become part of it can be deducted.

A deduction is also denied for expenditure on an item of capital nature which is incurred on or in connection with the provision, alteration of disposal of an asset for use in an ordinary residential rental property, subject to an exception for replacement of domestic items, the cost of which can be deducted on a like-for-like basis. For 2024/25 and earlier years, and ordinary residential rental property excludes a furnished holiday let to which special rules apply. These rules are abolished from 6 April 2025 and from that date furnished holiday lettings are treated in the same way as other residential lets.

Capital expenditure cannot be deducted where the accruals basis is used. Capital allowances may be available in limited cases.

15.7. Joining Or Leaving The Cash Basis

A landlord who is eligible for the cash basis can decide each year whether to use the cash basis or instead elect to use the accruals basis. Where a landlord joins or leaves the cash basis, some adjustments are needed to prevent items being double counted or falling out of account altogether.

15.8. Planning Tips

Where the cash basis applies by default, check this gives the best result, and elect for the accruals basis if this is better. Consider the timing of receipts and payments and their impact on the taxable profit.

16. Property Partnerships and Joint Ownership

16.1. Introduction to Tax Treatment of Jointly Owned Property

There are many scenarios in which property may be owned jointly, and joint ownership may arise for personal or commercial reasons. Where property is owned jointly, the way in which income arising from it is taxed will depend on whether or not there is a property partnership. Likewise the taxation of any gains on the disposal of the property will also depend on whether a property partnership exists. Owning property jointly does not in itself create a property partnership.

Where the joint ownership does not amount to a property partnership, the tax rules will depend on whether the co-owners are spouses or civil partners, or not. Special rules apply to determine the default income split where a rental property is jointly owned by spouse or civil partners.

Where a partnership exists, each owner will be taxable on their share of any profits, as determined in accordance with the property sharing ratio.

16.2. Is There A Partnership?

In determining the correct treatment of income from jointly owned property, the starting point is to ascertain whether or not a property partnership exists.

16.2.1. The Legal Definition Of A Partnership

A partnership is defined in the *Partnership Act* 1890, s. 1(1):
'Partnership is the relationship which subsists between persons carrying on a business in common with a view to profit'.

Companies are specifically excluded from the definition of a partnership.
However, s. 2 of the Act further provides the following rules for determining whether or not a partnership exists:

1. Joint tenancy, tenancy in common, joint property, common property or part ownership does not of itself create a partnership as to anything so held or owned, whether the tenants or owners do or do not share any profits made by the use thereof.

2. The sharing of gross returns does not of itself create a partnership, whether the persons sharing such returns have or have not a joint or common right or interest in any property from which or from the use of which the returns are derived.

3. The receipt of a person of a share of the profits or the business is *prima facie* evidence that he is a partner in the business, but the receipt of such a share, or of a payment contingent on or varying with the profits of a business, does not of itself make him a partner in the business; and in particular –

   a. The receipt by a person of a debt or other liquidated amount by instalments or otherwise out of the accruing profits of a business does not of itself make him a partner in the business or liable as such;

b. A contract for the remuneration of a servant or agent of a person engaged in a business by a share of the profits of the business does not of itself make the servant or agent a partner in the business or liable as such;

c. person being the widow, widower surviving civil partner or child of a deceased partner, and receiving by way of annuity a portion of the profits made in the business in which the deceased person was a partner, is not by reason only of such receipt a partner in the business or liable as such;

d. The advance of money by way of loan to a person engaged or about to engage in any business on a contract with that person that the lender shall receive a rate of interest varying with profits, or shall receive a share of the profits arising from carrying on the business does not of itself make the lender a partner with the person or persons carrying on the business or liable as such. Provided that the contract is in writing, and signed by or on behalf of all the parties thereto.

e. A person receiving by way of an annuity or otherwise a portion of the profits of a business in consideration of the sale by him of the goodwill in the business is not only by reason of such receipt a partner in the business or liable as such.'

By virtue of the *Partnership Act* 1890, s. 3, persons who enter into partnerships with one another are, for the purposes of that Act, called collectively a firm.

Different rules apply in Scotland and in Scotland a partnership is a separate legal entity. This is not the case in the rest of the UK; the partnership is transparent.

16.2.2. HMRC's Approach To Determining Whether A Partnership Exists

HMRC address the question of whether a partnership exists in their Partnership Manual at PM133000.

Their starting point is the definition in the *Partnership Act* 1890, s. 1.

HMRC advise their officers to establish all the facts to determine the true relationship between the parties, including the intention of the parties. They stress that no single factor is likely to be conclusive on its own – an overall view should be formed based on all the facts and evidence.

While the existence of a partnership agreement is not conclusive proof of the existence of a partnership, HMRC will accept the assertion that a partnership exists without supporting evidence, such as a partnership agreement.

It should also be noted that while the receipt of a share of the net profits suggests a partnership, an agreement to share net losses in the sense of being obliged to make good those losses is, in HMRC's view, a stronger indication of a partnership.

In a property context, HMRC make it clear in their Property Income Manual at PIM030 that:

'Joint letting does not, of itself, make the activity a partnership' and that usually where a property is jointly-owned there won't be a partnership, and a joint owner's share of the rental profits from the jointly-owned property will be included as part of their personal business rental profits. Less commonly, the joint letting will amount to a partnership. Where this is the case, the joint owners' shares of the rental profit must be kept separate from any other rental income.

They further stress that a partnership is unlikely to exist where a person is one of a group of joint partners who merely let property that they jointly own. By contrast, a partnership may exist where a person is one of a group of joint owners who let the property jointly and who provide additional services in return for payment. This may, for example, include the provision of property management services, or the provision of cleaning or gardening services. It is, in HMRC's view, the provision of the additional services that turn an investment activity (letting) into a business activity, and in doing so creates a partnership.

HMRC do not specify what additional services need to be provided to cross the boundary between an investment and running a business. However, they make it clear that in determining whether a partnership exists, 'much depends on the amount of business activity involved' and that the 'existence of a partnership depends on a degree of organisation similar to that required in an ordinary commercial business'. While letting a jointly-owned property through an agency would not qualify as running a business, actively managing a property portfolio – advertising for tenants, collecting rent, chasing debts, managing repairs, etc. – is likely to provide the degree of business activity necessary for a partnership.

HMRC's view is that where properties are jointly owned, the existence of a partnership is very much the exception rather than the rule. They state that 'most cases of jointly owned property will fall short of the degree of business organisation that is needed to constitute a partnership'. More is needed than deriving rental income from the letting of property – there must be a business apart from that.

Jointly owned properties may also be let out as part of a partnership business where a trading or professional partnership also lets some of its land or buildings, such as surplus office space. Where this is the case, the partnership can, in certain circumstances, choose for the rents from the temporary letting of surplus business accommodation to be included in the trading or professional profit.

Jointly owned properties may also be held by a partnership that runs an investment business which does not amount to a trade but which includes or consists of the letting of property.

Where a partnership already exists, and that partnership has income from property belonging to the partnership, HMRC's presumption is that the letting is part of the partnership business and is more than mere joint ownership.

16.2.3. Case Study 1 – Letting of Jointly-Owned Property: Is There A Partnership?

Andrew and Anthony are brothers. They jointly own several residential properties which they let out. They do not provide any other services.

In this situation, the absence of business activity means that there is no partnership – the fact that the properties are jointly-owned is not of itself sufficient to create a partnership.

Bert and Bernard are also brothers. They are in partnership as grocers and the partnership owns the premises from which the grocer's is run. There is a flat above the retail premises which is let out. The rental income forms part the income of the partnership.

Caroline and Christine are sisters. They jointly own five bungalows which they let to elderly people. In addition, they provide a number of services, including cleaning, gardening and shopping services. The provision of the services provides the additional business element to the letting of bungalows necessary for a partnership to exist.

16.3. Formation And Dissolution Of A Partnership

A partnership is formed by agreement. This does not have to be in writing and can be an oral agreement. However, it is usual to have a partnership agreement or deed in writing setting out the framework for running the partnership (see section 16.3.2).

16.3.1. When Does The Partnership Commence?

The date on which the partnership commences is a question of fact.

If a partnership is formed by an oral agreement, it will commence when the terms of that oral agreement are implemented. This is the case even if the terms are later formally executed in writing.

Where there is no prior oral agreement, the creation of a written partnership agreement or deed creates a partnership. However, a written agreement cannot create a partnership with retrospective effect.

16.3.2. The Partnership Agreement

There is no legal requirement for there to be a written partnership agreement or partnership deed. As noted at 16.3.1 above, a partnership can be formed by oral agreement. However, it is prudent to have a written agreement setting out, for the avoidance of doubt or disagreement, the rights and responsibilities of each partner. The partnership agreement is a legal contract.

There is no one size fits all – the partnership agreement should be tailored to the specific needs of the particular partnership. However, a partnership agreement will typically cover some or all of the following:

- The responsibilities of each partner.
- Each partner's ownership share.
- The way in which profits and losses are to be shared.
- The capital contribution required from each partner.
- The process for admitting new partners.
- How decisions are to be made.
- What happens when a partner leaves/retires or dies.
- The name of the nominated partner.

The words 'Partnership Agreement' should be clearly stated on the document, which should be signed and dated by all the partners.

16.3.3. Dissolution Of A Partnership

As a partnership is the relationship between a particular combination of partners, any changes in those persons terminates that partnership. This may or may not result in the creation of a new partnership. Whether a new partnership is created depends on the facts in each case.

16.3.4. Case Study 2 – Dissolution Of A Partnership – Is A New Partnership Created?

David and Deborah jointly own a property and provide property management services. They are in partnership together. David leaves the partnership, but Deborah continues to run the business. The partnership is dissolved and Deborah operates as a sole trader. However, she finds the workload too much and six months later goes into partnership with Dawn. A new partnership is created.

Evan, Emma and Eunice are also in partnership together. Evan leaves the partnership, but Emma and Eunice continue to run the business. The original partnership comprising Evan, Emma and Eunice is dissolved when Evan leaves, but a new partnership comprising Emma and Eunice is created on the same day.

A partnership may also be dissolved on the occurrence of a particular event. This may include the death or bankruptcy of a partner. A partnership may also be created for a specific venture and be dissolved when that venture comes to an end. A partner may also give notice to his or her fellow partners of their intention to dissolve the partnership.

From a legislative perspective, the law governing the dissolution of a partnership is found in the *Partnership Act* 1890, ss. 32—35.

16.3.5. Change Of Partners – Partnership Treated As Continuing For Tax Purposes

Under partnership law, where there is a change in partners, the original partnership is treated as coming to an end and, if the remaining partners continue in business, either alone or with a new partner, a new partnership is treated as having been formed.

However, for tax purposes, the partnership is treated as continuing where there is a change in the partners as long as there is a least one partner who was a member of the partnership both before and after the change. This prevents cessation and commencement rules from being triggered each time there is a change in the members of a partnership.

16.4. Taxation Of Partnership Profits

Although the profit or loss for the partnership is computed at partnership level, a partnership is transparent for tax purposes. The profit or loss is allocated to the partners in accordance with the agreed profit sharing ratio and each partner is charged to tax on their share of the profits. Where the partner is an individual, their share of the partnership's profits is charged to income tax and must be notified to HMRC on the partnership pages of their self-assessment tax return. Their income tax liability is computed by reference to their total taxable income (including their share of partnership profits), less relevant allowances and reliefs. Individuals are also liable to Class 4 National Insurance on their partnership profits where these exceed the lower profits limit (£12,570 for 2024/25). The liability to Class 2 contributions is abolished from 6 April 2024. However, where the partner's share of the profits is below the small profits threshold, (£6,725 for 2024/25) they can make voluntary Class 2 contributions to secure a qualifying year for state pension purposes. This is cheaper than paying Class 3 National Insurance contributions. A National Insurance credit is awarded where profits are between the small profits threshold and lower profits limit, providing the partner with a qualifying year for state pension purposes..

If the partner has any corporate partners, their share of the partnership profits is charged to corporation tax.

Each individual partner is responsible for filing a self-assessment or corporation tax return, as appropriate. In addition, the partnership must file a partnership tax return, providing HMRC with details of the partnership's income and related information. This must be filed online by 31 January after the end of the tax year to which it relates (or by 31 October after the end of the tax year if a paper return is filed).

16.4.1. Separate Property Rental Businesses

If an individual is a member of a partnership which lets a property and that individual also lets property which they own in an individual capacity (or a joint capacity outside the partnership), the individual will have two property rental businesses. This distinction is important as losses from a property rental business can only be carried forward and set against future profits of the same property rental business. It is not possible to set losses from property partnership against the profits of an individual property rental business, and vice versa.

16.4.2. Case Study – Separate Property Rental Businesses

Freddie own two flats which he lets out. He is also a partner in a partnership which lets out units to other businesses.

Freddie is treated as running two property rental businesses:
1. His own property rental business comprising the two flats.
2. The partnership rental property business comprising the let units.

Freddie must keep his profits or losses from the partnership rental property business separate from the profits or losses of his personal property business, and declare them separately on his tax return.

16.5. Why Form A Property Partnership?

As noted previously, the fact that a property is jointly-owned is not enough in itself to create a partnership – there must also be a sufficient degree of business activity. However, there are definite advantages to operating as a partnership where property is jointly owned, the main one being the flexibility as to how profits and losses are allocated.

Where property is jointly owned outside a property partnership, there are strict rules on how the income is allocated to the joint owners for tax purposes. Where the joint owners are not married or in a civil partnership, the default position is that profits and losses are shared in accordance with their ownership shares; although there is some flexibility to agree a different split. The treatment of joint owners who are not in partnership and who are not spouses or civil partner is discussed in more detail in section 16.6.

However, where the joint owners are spouses or civil partners, the default position is that income is shared 50:50 regardless of the underlying ownership (see 16.7.1). While there is the option to elect for income to be shared in accordance with actual underlying beneficial ownership where this is other than 50:50 (see section 16.8.6), other profit in allocations are not permitted. In a partnership situation, the partners can agree to share profits in whatever way they like. This is very useful from a tax planning perspective as where the partners are spouses or civil partners it allows profits to be allocated in a way which minimises the partners' joint tax liability. Where the partners' other income varies from year-to-year, the partners can simply agree to share profits 'in such ratio as is agreed between the partners'. This will provide flexibility to tailor the allocation of profits each year to achieve the most favourable tax outcome.

In a partnership situation, partners can also use salaries to change the amount that each partner receives. This too can be used as a tax planning tool.

16.5.1. Case Study 3 – Advantages Of A Property Partnership

George and Grace are married. They have a number of properties that they own jointly and let out as residential lets. They also provide property management services, advertising for tenants, agreeing the tenancy, undertaking repairs and maintenance, and suchlike. They satisfy the business test necessary for there to be a partnership, and operate the business as the partnership.

To provide maximum flexibility, the partnership agreement provides that 'profits and losses will shared in such ratio as is agreed between the partners.

In 2023/24, the partnership made a profits of £60,000. George works outside the partnership and had a salary of £70,000. Grace takes a salary of £12,570 from the partnership, equal to her personal allowance for 2023/24.

As Grace has her basic rate band available, it make sense for the couple to make use of this. Consequently, they agree for 2023/24 to share the profits in the ratio 3:1, with Grace having 75% of the profits and George having the remaining 25%.

Grace is taxed on her share of the partnership profits of £45,000 on which she pays tax of £10,460 ((£37,700 @ 20%) + (£7,300 @ 40%)). George receives profits of £15,000 on which he pays tax of £6,000 (£15,000 @ 40%). Their combined tax bill on the partnership profits is £16,460.

Had Grace and George not been in a partnership, the profits would have been split equally for tax purposes and they would each have paid tax on profits of £30,000. This would give Grace a tax bill of £6,000 (£30,000 @ 20%) and George a tax bill of £12,000 (£30,000 @ 40%). Their combined tax bill would be £18,000. By being in partnership and having the flexibility to share profits other than 50:50, they are able to utilise all of Grace's basic rate band and save tax of £1,540.

On 6 April 2024, George retires from his other job. In that year, his only income is a salary from the partnership of £12,570 equal to his personal allowance. Grace also has a salary from the partnership of £12,570 and other income from a new rental property that she owns in her sole name of £17,700. The partnership profits are again £60,000. However, this year, they agree to share profits in the ration 1:2, with Grace having 1/3 of the profits and George having 2/3. Grace receives profits of £20,000 which use up her remaining basic rate band (£37,700 - £17,700) and on which she pays tax of £4,000. George receives profits of £40,000, on which he pays tax of £8,460 ((£37,700 @ 20%) + (£2,300 @ 40%)). Their combined tax bill on the partnership profits is £12,460. Had profits been allocated evenly, Grace would have paid tax of £8,000 on her £30,000 share and George would have paid tax of £6,000 on his £30,000 – a combined tax bill of £14,000. By being able to choose the profit split they are able to reduce their combined tax bill by £1,540.

Operating as partnership provides the flexibility to allocate profits other than equally or in accordance with the underlying beneficial ownership where different. By not having a fixed profit sharing ratio, a partnership also allows the partners to change the profit share ratio each year as circumstances change in order to secure the best tax outcome.

16.6. Joint Ownership Outside A Partnership

As previously noted, where property is owned jointly, in most cases there will not be a partnership as the necessary business element will not be present. Consequently, the letting will usually be regarded as an investment activity.

Where jointly owned property is let out, some of the tax implications depend on the relationship between the joint owners.

16.6.1. Joint Tenants And Tenants In Common

Under English property law, there are two ways in which property can be owned jointly – as joint tenants and as tenants in common. The way in which a jointly owned property is owned has implications for what each owner can do with their share and dictates what happens should one of them die. It also has other tax implications.

16.6.2. Joint Tenants

Where a property is owned as joint tenants, the owners together own all of the property equally – together they own the whole rather than each owning a specified share. When one owner dies, the remaining owner(s) continue to own the whole property. The deeds are changed to the names of the surviving co-owner or owners once a death certificate has been provided to Land Registry.

Spouses and civil partners generally opt to own property together as joint tenants to ensure that it passes to the surviving spouse or civil partner on death. However, from a tax perspective, this is not always the best option, particularly in relation to an investment property which is let out to provide an income.

16.6.3. Tenants In Common

The other option for owning property jointly is as tenants in common. Where this route is taken, each joint owner owns a specified share of the property. That share is theirs to do with it what they choose. On death, their share is distributed in accordance with their Will (or under the intestacy rules where there is no Will) – it does not pass automatically to the other joint owners.

Ownership as tenants in common is popular where the joint owners are not in a relationship, for example, if a group of friends buy a property together. However, it can also be beneficial for married couples and civil partners to own property as tenants in common, rather than as joint tenants, as it allows for an element of flexibility when tax planning which is not available where a property is owned as joint tenants.

Where property is owned as tenants in common and the ownership shares are not specified, the owners are deemed to own the property in equal shares.

16.7. Joint Owners Who Are Not Spouses Or Civil Partners

Where there is no partnership and property is jointly owned by persons who are not spouses or civil partners, for income tax purposes, each person is taxed on their own share of the profits and, if there is a loss, each person has their own share of the loss to carry forward and set against future profits from the same property rental business. It must be remembered that only property owned in the same capacity can be within the same property rental business. This means that if a person owns property both jointly and on their own, the income from the jointly-owned property is treated separately for tax purposes from that from the property owned in an individual capacity – losses from one stream cannot be set against profits of the other.

16.7.1. Default Position – Profits And Losses Allocated In Ownership Shares

As a general rule, where property is jointly owned outside a partnership by persons who are not spouses or civil partner, profits and losses are normally allocated in accordance with the joint owners' ownership share in the property.

16.7.2. Case Study 4 – Profits Allocated In Ownership Share

Harry, Helen and Hugo are siblings who own a property together which they let out. Harry owns 40% of the property and Helen and Hugo each own 30%.

In 2024/25, they make a profit of £20,000 from letting out the property.

The profits are allocated in the ratio 40:30:30 in accordance with the share that they each have in the ownership of the property. Consequently, Harry receives £8,000, Helen receives £6,000 and Hugo receives £6,000. Each is taxed on the profits that they actually receive.

16.7.3. A Different Allocation

A split of profits in accordance with underlying ownership shares will not always give the best result for tax purposes, and where the joint owners are not married or in a civil partnership they can choose to share profits or losses in a way that is different to their ownership shares in the property. This situation is more likely to arise where the joint owners are in a relationship and have combined finances, but are not married or in a civil partnership.

Where profits and losses are allocated in different proportions to the underlying ownership share, each person is taxed on the profits that they actually receive. It is not possible to agree a split purely for tax purposes, but actually share profits in accordance with the underlying ownership. The share for tax purposes must be the share agreed and the share that each owner actually receives.

Case Study 5 – Allocation Other Than In Relation To Ownership Shares

Ian and Iona are an unmarried couple. They have been together for several years and have a baby daughter. They jointly own a property which they let out. They own the property as tenants in common. Ian has a 60% share and Iona has a 40% share.

In 2024/25, the rental income from the property is £16,000.

Ian has a job in IT in which he earns £45,000. Iona does not work and has no other income.

To ensure that Iona's personal allowance is not wasted, they agree to split the income in the ratio 8:2, with Iona receiving 80% of the rental profits and Ian receiving 20% of rental profits. Consequently, Iona receives rental profits of £12,800 and Ian receives rental profits of £3,200.

Iona's share of the profits is mostly covered by her personal allowance of £12,570, leaving £230 in charge on which she pays tax of £46 (£230 @ 20%). Ian pays tax of £640 on his share of the profits (£3,200 @ 20%). Their combined tax bill is £686.

If they had allocated the profits in accordance with their ownership shares in the property, Ian would have received profits of £9,600 (60% of £16,000) on which he would pay tax of £2,876 ((£5,720 @ 20%) + (£4,330 @ 40%)). Iona would receive profits of £6,400 (40% of £16,000) on which no tax would be payable as her share of her profits would be sheltered by her personal allowance. In this situation, their combined tax bill would be £2,786 – an additional £2,190 compared to a 20:80 split. Sharing profits in accordance with the ownership share would mean that £6,170 of Iona's personal allowance is wasted; income which instead is taxed in Ian's hands, some of which being taxed at 40%.

16.8. Joint Owners Are Spouses And Civil Partners

Although, there are a number of tax breaks available to spouses and civil partners where property is owned jointly outside a partnership, they lack the flexibility which is available to unmarried sharers to choose how to share profits and losses. In this regard, the tax rules can be quite restrictive, although planning opportunities do exist.

These rules do not apply to furnished holiday lettings, which are discussed at 16.8.8.

16.8.1. Default Position – Profits And Losses Allocated 50:50

Where property is jointly owned by a married couple or by civil partners, any rental income is treated as accruing to them jointly regardless of whether their actual beneficial ownership is different. This may not always be the best option from a tax perspective. However, it can also create some tax planning opportunities.

16.8.2. Case Study 6 – Income Allocated 50:50

Jack and Joanna have been married for several years. They jointly own a rental property as joint tenants. For 2024/25, the rental profit from the property is £20,000. Joanna is an additional rate taxpayer. Jack works part time earning £15,000 a year. Neither has any other income other than the rental income.

The rental profit is deemed to be allocated to them in equal shares for tax purposes, so Joanna is treated as receiving £10,000 and Jack is treated as receiving £10,000. Consequently, as an additional rate taxpayer, Joanna pays tax at 45% on her share – a tax bill of £4,500, and as a basic rate taxpayer, Jack pays tax at 20% on his share – a tax bill of £2,000. Their combined tax bill is £6,500.

This is not ideal from a tax perspective. It would be better for them to be able to choose for Jack to receive all the rental profit to make use of his available basic rate band. This would reduce the tax on the rental income to £4,000, saving them tax of £2,500.

However, as they are married, this option is not available to them and the profit is allocated on a 50:50 basis. As they own the property as joint tenants, the option of making a Form 17 election (see section 16.8.4) is not available to them either.

16.8.3. Case Study 7 – Taking Advantage Of The 50:50 Income Allocation Rule

Karl and Karen have been married for several years. They jointly own a property which they let out. The property is owned as tenants in common. Karl has a 95% share and Karen has a 5% share.

In 2024/25 the rental profits from letting the property are £30,000.

Karen works part time and has a salary of £14,000.

Karl work full-time and has a salary of £80,000.

Despite the unequal beneficial ownership of the property, the income is split 50:50 for tax purposes, such that Karl and Karen are both treated as having rental profits of £15,000.

Karen pays tax of £3,000 (£15,000 @ 20%) on her share and Karl pays tax of £6,000 (£15,000 @ 40%) on his share). Their combined tax bill is £9,000.

Had the income been allocated in accordance with their ownership shares, Karl would have been taxed on rental profits of £28,500 (95% of £30,000) on which he would have paid tax of £11,400 (£28,000 @ 40%) and Karen would have been taxed on rental profits of £1,500 (5% of £30,000) on which she would have paid tax of £300 (£1,500 @ 20%). This would have given rise to a combined tax bill of £11,700 - £2,700 more than that arising by virtue of the deemed 50:50 allocation. In this instance, the 50:50 split provides a favourable result.

16.8.4. Putting A Property In Joint Names To Take Advantage Of The 50:50 Income Allocation?

Spouses and civil partners are able to transfer assets between them at a value that give rise to neither a gain nor a loss. This can be used to take advantage of the deemed 50:50 income allocation rule to transfer income from one spouse or civil partner to reduce the overall tax bill, but without the transferor having to give away/sell a 50% stake in the asset.

16.8.5. Case Study 8 – Putting a Proeprty In Joint Name To Take Advantage Of 50:50 Income Allocation Rule

Louise has a rental property which is owned in her sole name. She pays tax at 40%. Her civil partner, Lisa, works part time earning £13,000 a year.

At the start of the tax year, Louise transfers a 5% stake in the property to Lisa, retaining a 95% stake. The property is owned as tenants in common. The couple take advantage of the no gain/no loss rule to make the transfer at a value that gives rise to neither a gain nor a loss. Consequently, there is no capital gains tax to pay.

For 2024/25, the rental profits is £20,000.

By making the transfer, the property is now jointly owned and the income is deemed to be allocated 50:50. Consequently, Louise is taxed on rental profits of £10,000, and pays tax of £4,000 on those profits, and Lisa is taxed on profits of £10,000, paying tax of £2,000 on those profits. The combined tax bill is £6,000.

Had the property remained in Louise's sole name, she would have paid tax of £8,000 on the profits. By transferring a small stake to Lisa, the couple are able to reduce the tax bill on the rental profits by 25%.

The deemed 50:50 allocation rule means that Louise can retain a 95% share in the property, but effectively transfer 50% of the income to Lisa for tax purposes.

16.8.6. Unequal Ownership Shares And A Form 17 Election

As noted in section 16.7.1 above, where married couples or civil partners own property jointly, any income from that property is treated for tax purposes as accruing to them in equal shares and each spouse/civil partner is taxed on 50% of the income. This will not always produce the most desirable result from a tax perspective.

However, where the property is owned as tenants in common in unequal shares, the couple can make a Form 17 election for the income to be allocated for tax purposes in accordance with their underlying ownership shares. A Form 17 election is only possible where the property is owned as tenants in common in unequal shares; where the property is owned as joint tenants, the owners jointly own the whole property equally. Thus, to be able to take advantage of a Form 17 election, married couples and civil partners may wish to own joint rental properties as tenants in common.

Form 17 can be found on the Gov.uk website at www.gov.uk/government/publications/income-tax-declaration-of-beneficial-interests-in-joint-property-and-income-17.

Where a Form 17 election is made, it must reach HMRC within 60 days of the date of the last signature for it to be valid. The election will not apply if it is received by HMRC outside this timescale. Income is treated as arising in accordance with the underlying beneficial ownership from the date of the Form 17 election – income received prior to the date of the election is treated as arising equally. Thus, if a couple wish for the rental income for the tax year to be allocated in accordance with the actual ownership of the property, the election must be made at the start of the tax year. If it is not made until the end of the tax year, it will not achieve its desired effect.

The timing rules means that it is not possible to wait until after the end of the tax year and see what income each party has received and then decide whether the election would be beneficial or not. This could be problematic if income is uncertain and it is not possible to know in advance whether the election will be beneficial, what actually happens may be very different from what one expects to happen. A Form 17 election cannot apply retrospectively.

Married couples and civil partners can make use of the no gain/no loss rules applying for capital gains tax purposes to change the actual ownership of the property to prior making a Form 17 election to achieve the desired income split. Making a Form 17 election is only worthwhile if the combined tax bill is lower than if the income is allocated 50:50 for tax purposes.

16.8.7. Case Study 9 – Benefits Of Making A Form 17 Election

Mark and Mary have been married for a number of years. They invest in a rental property which they own as tenants in common with Mark owing a 20% stake and Mary owning an 80% stake.

In March 2024, Mary retires and in 2024/25, she expects to receive pension income of £13,000.

Mark continues to work, remaining a higher rate taxpayer.

Prior to the start of the 2024/25 tax year, they make a Form 17 election. As a result, the rental profits for the year of £40,000 are allocated in accordance with their beneficial ownership shares, so that Mary is taxed on 80% (£32,000) on which she pays tax of £6,400 (£32,000 @ 20%), while Mark is taxed on £8,000 (20%) on which he pays tax of £3,200 (£8,000 @ 40%). Their combined tax bill is £9,600.

In the absence of the Form 17 election, they would each have been taxed on rental profits of £20,000, with Mark paying tax of £8,000 (£20,000 @ 40%) and Mary paying tax of £4,000 (£20,000 @ 20%). This would give them a combined tax bill of £12,000.

Making the Form 17 election saves the couple £2,400 in tax.

16.8.8. Special Rules For Furnished Holiday Lettings

For 2024/25 and earlier tax years, a special tax regime applies to furnished holiday lettings. This regime is abolished from 6 April 2025.

For 2024/25 and earlier tax years. rules outlined above do not apply where a jointly let property qualifies as a furnished holiday letting for tax purposes, with the result that where the property is jointly owned by spouses or civil partners, the income is not treated as being allocated equally for tax purposes. Instead, the parties can choose how to allocate the income, so can do this in the way that minimises their combined tax bill. The ability for the parties to decide how to split the rental profits applies regardless of whether the joint owners are married or in a civil partnership or not.

From 2025/26 consequent on the abolition of the special tax regime for furnished holiday lettings, the rules outlined above will apply to furnished holiday lettings as they apply to other let property which is jointly-owned.

16.9. Other Tax Considerations

Where a landlord owns property jointly, the tax considerations are not limited to securing the best result as regards the taxation of the rental income.

16.9.1. Capital Gains Tax

As already discussed, married couples and civil partners can take advantage of the no gain/no loss rule which allows them to transfer assets between them without triggering a capital gain to change the underlying ownership shares of a rental property in order to reduce the tax payable on the rental income (see sections 16.7.1 and 16.8.6).

Married couples and civil partners can also make use of this rule to change the ownership prior to sale to take advantage of a spouse's or civil partner's unused annual exempt amount or basic rate band.

For capital gains tax purposes, each owner is taxed on their share of the gain. Where the property is owned as joint tenants, the gain is split equally for tax purposes. Thus, if a buy-to-let property owned by a married couple as tenants in common is sold, each spouse would be taxed on 50% of the gain. For unmarried couples, the gain would also arise evenly.

Where the property is owned as tenants in common, the gain arises in relation to the beneficial shares. This is the case regardless of whether or not the owners are married or in a civil partnership; there is no deemed 50:50 split for capital gains tax purposes as for income tax purposes. However, where the current underlying beneficial ownership does not give the best result for capital gains tax purposes, the couple can change this prior to sale, taking advantage of the no gain/no loss rule.

It should be noted that what may be the optimal ownership split for income tax purposes may not be the same for capital gains tax purposes, and the position should be reviewed prior to sale.

Where a property partnership exists, any capital gains on the sale of partnership assets are allocated to the partners in accordance with the partnership agreement. These are chargeable on the partner personally, taken together with any personal gains/allowable losses in the same tax year.

16.9.2. Case Study 10 – Making Use Of The No Gain/No Loss Rule Prior To Sale

Nigel and Nina are married and own a rental property as tenants in common, with Nina owning 5% of the property and Nigel owning 95% of the property. They plan to sell the property before the end of the 2024/25 tax year and expect to realise a gain of £100,000.

Nina has already used her annual exempt amount. She has £35,000 of her basic rate band remaining available.

Nigel is a higher rate taxpayer. He has not used his annual exempt amount for 2024/25 and is a higher rate taxpayer. The annual exempt amount for 2024/25 is set at £3,000.

With the current ownership split, Nina will be taxed on £5,000 of the gain on which capital gains tax of £900 will be payable (£5,000 @ 18%) and Nigel will be taxed on £95,000 of the gain on which tax of £22,080 ((£95,000 - £3,000) @ 24%) will be payable. The combined capital gains tax bill will be £22,980.

However, if they take advantage of the no gain/no loss rule to transfer a further 30% share to Nina prior to sale (so that Nina owns 35% and Nigel owns 65%), Nina will be taxed on £35,000 of the gain on which capital gains tax of £6,300 (£35,000 @ 18%) will be payable and Nigel will be taxed on £65,000 of the gain on which capital gains tax of £14,880 ((£65,000 - £3,000) @ 24%) will be payable, a combined bill of £21,180. By changing the ownership shares prior to sale, the couple are able to make full use of Nigel's annual exempt amount and Nina's remaining basic rate band, reducing their combined capital gains tax bill to £21,180, saving them £1,800.

16.9.3. SDLT, LBTT And LTT

Where a property is owned jointly by two or more people (either as joint tenants or as tenants in common) and the property is divided physically and equally so that each person owns a separate share, there is no SDLT (LBTT in Scotland, LTT in Wales) to pay. However, if one person takes a bigger share, or takes over the whole property, and the consideration is over the relevant threshold, SDLT (or LBTT/LTT as appropriate) will be payable.

Where spouses or civil partners take advantage of the no gain/no loss rule to change the underlying ownership, if there is no consideration, no SDLT (or LBTT/LTT) will be payable. However, it should be remembered that consideration includes taking over a share of the mortgage and where the mortgage taken over exceeds the relevant threshold, SDLT (or LBTT/LTT) will be payable.

16.9.4. Inheritance Tax

Regardless of whether the property is owned as joint tenants or as tenants in common, the deceased's share forms part of their estate. However, under the survivorship rules, where a property is owned as joint tenants it automatically passes to the surviving joint owners on death. Thus, where a property is owned by spouses or civil partners as joint tenants, it will automatically pass to the surviving spouse or civil partner on death and benefit from the spouse exemption. If the joint owners are not spouses or civil partners, the property will still pass to the remaining joint owners if one joint owner dies.

By contrast, where property is owned as tenants in common, the deceased's share will pass in accordance with their Will (or under intestacy laws where there is no Will). If it is left to the surviving spouse, it will benefit from the spouse exemption. Where it is left to a beneficiary other than a spouse or civil partner, the nil rate band will be available (as will the residence nil rate band where the property is the deceased's main residence and is left to children or other direct descendants). This can be an attractive option to shelter the property against care costs, or where property prices are expected to increase faster than any rise in the nil rate band.

Consideration should be given as to how joint property is held and the preferred outcome on the death of a joint owner.

Companies And Property Taxes

17. Should Landlords Operate Through A Limited Company

Unincorporated landlords have been hard hit by a series of tax changes in recent years, including the gradual restriction in tax relief for mortgage and finance costs for residential lets, meaning that relief is now only available as a tax reduction given at the basic rate. As this restriction does not apply to companies, a natural question is whether it is better for a landlord to operate through a limited company.

As with many questions, the answer is 'it depends'. Whether operating through a limited company is a more tax-efficient option will depend on a number of factors including:

- whether the landlord has an existing portfolio or is a new landlord;
- the rate at which the landlord pays income tax;
- the rate at which the company pays corporation tax;
- the amount of profit the landlord will need to withdraw from the company for personal use;
- whether the landlord lets, or is planning to let, residential, furnished holiday or commercial properties,
- the level of borrowings that the landlord has; and the tax and other costs of transferring an existing portfolio into a limited company.

17.1. Pros And Cons Of Operating Through A Limited Company

As with most things in life, there are advantages and disadvantages to operating through a limited company. These are considered below.

In deciding whether operating through a limited company is more beneficial, it is necessary to weigh up the advantages and the disadvantages, and crunch the numbers.

17.1.1. Advantages

One of the main advantages of operating as limited company is that finance costs and interest are fully deductible in computing profits, rather than relief being given as a tax reduction. This is a significant driver to incorporation.

Profits made by a company are chargeable to corporation tax. From 1 April 2023 onwards, companies with profits not exceeding the lower limit (set at £50,000 for a standalone company) pay corporation tax at 19%. Where profits exceed the upper limit (set at £250,000 for a standalone company), corporation tax is charged at 25%. Where profits fall between the lower limit and the upper limit, corporation tax is charged at the rate of 25% as reduced by marginal relief. This result in an effective rate of corporation tax of between 19% and 25% depending where in the band the company's profits fall.

Marginal relief is found by the formula:

F x (U-A) x N/A

Where:
- F is the marginal relief fraction (set at 3/200 for the financial year 2023);
- U is the upper limit;
- A is the amount of augmented profits (profits plus dividends from non-group companies); and
- N is the amount of total taxable profits.

If the company does not have any dividends from non-group companies, N is equal to A and N/A is equal to 1. Where this is the case, the formula can be simplified to F x (U- A).

The profits are taxed at 19% up to the lower profits limit, at 26.5% between the lower profits limit and the upper profits limit and at 25% on profits in excess of the upper profits limit.

Example

A standalone company has profits for the year to 31 March 2024 of £100,000. It has no dividend income.

The company is eligible for marginal relief of 3/200 x (£250,000 - £100,000) = £2,250.

The company will pay corporation tax of £22,750 ((£100,000 @ 25%) - £2,250).

This is equivalent to (£50,000 @ 19%) + (£50,000 @ 26.5%) (£9,500 + £13,250 = £22,750).

Where the company has one or more associated companies, the lower and upper limits are divided by the number of associated companies plus 1. The following table shows the limits where the number of associated companies ranges from 0 to 5.

Number of associates	Lower limit	Upper limit
0	£50,000	£250,000
1	£25,000	£125,000
2	£16,667	£83,333
3	£12,500	£62,500
4	£10,000	£50,000
5	£8,333	£41,447

The limits are also proportionately reduced if the accounting period is less than 12 months.

The rate of corporation tax is significantly lower than the higher and additional rates of income tax, as the maximum rate of corporation tax will be 25%, compared to the higher rate of income tax at 40% and the additional rate of income tax at 45%. Further, the small profits rate of 19% is less than the basic rate of income tax of 20%.

On the sale of a property held by a company, any chargeable gain is taxed to corporation tax. However, following the reduction in the higher residential rate of capital gains tax from 28% to 24% with effect from 6 April 2024, where the property is a residential property, the rate of corporation tax (at a maximum of 25%) is more than the rate of capital gains tax payable by individual landlords whose income and gains exceed the basic, who will pay capital gains tax on residential property gains at the rate of 24% and at the rate of 20% on non-residential gains. Where the effective rate of corporation tax is less than 24%, the rate at which corporation tax is charged on the gain will be less than the rate of capital gains tax paid by a landlord on residential gains where income and gains exceed the basic rate band; similarly, where the effective rate of corporation tax is less than 20%, this will be less than the capital gains tax paid by a landlord who is a higher rate taxpayer on non-residential gains. Where the landlords' income and gains fall with the basic rate band, the landlord will pay capital gains tax at the lower residential rate of 18%. This is lower than the small profits rate.

Unlike individuals, companies do not need to notify HMRC of residential property gains within 60 days and make a payment on account of the tax due on the gain within the same timescale. This provides a cash flow advantage as tax on the gain is not payable until nine months and one day after the end of the accounting period in which the gain was realised.

On the downside, companies do not benefit from an annual exempt amount. However, the advantage of this is diminishing as the annual exempt amount fell from £12,300 for 2022/23 to £6,000 for 2023/24, and again to £3,000 for 2024/25.

Operating as company also offers the added attraction of limited liability. In summary, the following advantages are available to landlords operating through a limited company:
- corporation tax (at between 19% and 25%) is paid on profits rather than income tax (at 20%, 40% or 45%);
- finance costs are fully deductible in computing profits;
- chargeable gains are taxable to corporation tax rather than to capital gains tax. This is advantageous where the company's effective rate of corporation tax is less than 24% and the landlord pays capital gains tax at the higher residential rate or where the effective rate is less than 20% and the landlord pays capital gains tax at 20% on non-residential gains.
- the company has limited liability.

17.1.2. Disadvantages

Despite the obvious attractions of operating as limited company, as listed above, there are disadvantages too. One of the main disadvantages is the potential tax charge that may arise when profits are extracted from the company. As the company is a separate legal person, distinct from the shareholders who own it, if the shareholders wish to use the profits personally, rather than leave them in the company, they will need to be extracted. This may give rise to a personal tax liability on the recipient, and possibly a National Insurance liability for both the company and the recipient if profits are taken as a salary.

Unlike an individual, a company does not have a personal allowance, so all profits are taxed. Companies cannot benefit from the £1,000 property allowance available to unincorporated landlords.

Similarly, there is no annual exempt amount for capital gains (set at £3,000 for 2024/25), so any gain is taxable in full. If the gain falls in the basic rate band, the rate (at 18% for residential gains or 10% for non-residential gains) is lower than the rate of corporation tax (which is between 19% and 25%). For non-residential gains, the top rate of capital gains tax is 20%, whereas, depending on the level of the company's profits, the rate of corporation tax charged on the gains may exceed 20%. Where the gain is on a residential property, the top residential rate of capital gains tax is 24%, which may be lower than the effective rate of corporation tax payable on the gain. Any personal capital losses cannot be set against a gain arising on the disposal of a property held by a company. Where an individual realises losses on other assets, such as shares, these can be set against a personal chargeable gain on the sale of the property.

There is also the issue of the annual tax on enveloped dwellings to consider where residential property is held by a limited company and the company is unable to benefit from any of the available reliefs or exemptions. The ATED is considered in Section 17.8 below.

Where the landlord already has a property portfolio, the up-front tax costs of transferring the property to a limited company can be significant.

The need to file accounts at Companies House and file a confirmation statement annually, as well as the costs of setting up a limited company, will mean the administrative costs of operating as a limited company are likely to be higher than for an unincorporated property company.

In summary, the potential disadvantages of operating a property business as a limited company are as follows:

- need to extract profits and associated tax and National Insurance liabilities;
- lack of personal allowance;
- no annual exempt amount for capital gains tax;
- potentially higher charges on capital gains;
- no property income allowance;
- potential ATED charge;
- higher administration costs;
- high up-front costs if incorporating an existing property business.

17.2. Incorporating An Existing Property Business

Landlords with existing property portfolios may wonder whether it may be beneficial to incorporate their business. However, as the existing properties have to be transferred to the limited company, there will be stamp duty land tax (land and building transaction tax in Scotland, land transaction tax in Wales) and capital gains tax implications.

These are considered below.

17.2.1. Stamp Duty Land Tax (SDLT)

The stamp duty land tax (SDLT) implications of transferring properties into a limited company are considered here. SDLT applies to properties in England and Northern Ireland. Similar considerations apply for land and buildings transaction tax (LBTT) to properties in Scotland and for land transaction tax (LTT) for properties in Wales.

One of the main disadvantages of incorporating an existing property business is that SDLT has to be paid again. Where the property is residential property, the 3% supplement applies if the consideration is £40,000 or more, meaning that the SDLT hit of incorporating a property business is likely to be significant.

If the property transferred is a commercial property, SDLT is payable at the commercial SDLT ratesMixed use properties are charged at the commercial rates.

Where a property is transferred to a connected company (as would be the case where a landlord transfers a property to a company and some or all of the consideration is in shares), the chargeable consideration for SDLT purposes is the market value of the property at the time that it was transferred.

If the properties have increased significantly in value since they were acquired by the landlord, the SDLT on transferring them to a limited company may be significantly more than the SDLT paid when the properties were originally acquired.

17.2.2. Capital Gains Tax (CGT)

As the landlord is disposing of properties owned personally to the limited company, there is a disposal for capital gains tax purposes. Further, as the disposal is to a connected company, the disposal is deemed to be at market value.

However, while a gain may arise, the existence of incorporation relief will mean that the tax on the gain is not payable until the landlord sells his or her shares in the company, which may not be for a very long time, if ever.

17.2.3. Incorporation Relief

Incorporation relief is available where a sole trader or partner in a business partnership transfers their business and all its assets (or all its assets except for cash) to a limited company in exchange for shares in that company.

The relief is given automatically – it does not have to be claimed.

The effect of the relief is to reduce the base cost of the shares by the capital gain on the property when it was transferred to the company. So if a landlord transfers property to a limited company in exchange for shares valued at £500,000, and realises a gain of £200,000 in doing so, the base cost of the shares is reduced by the held-over gain of £200,000 to £300,000. The gain does not crystallise until the shares are sold.

If the consideration is partly in share and partly in cash, incorporation relief only applies to that part of the consideration received in shares. The gain relating to consideration received in cash is immediately chargeable. So, if a landlord transfers property valued at £500,000 to a limited company in exchange for shares worth £400,000 and cash of £100,000, realising a gain of £100,000 in the process, 80% of the gain (£80,000) benefits from incorporation relief, reducing the base cost of the shares to £320,000. The remaining 20% of the gain (£20,000) is immediately chargeable to capital gains tax. However, this may be part sheltered by the annual exempt amount, where available. However, for 2024/25 this is now only £3,000.

17.2.4. Disclaim Incorporation Relief Where No CGT Payable

As incorporation relief is given automatically where the conditions for the relief are met, if the relief is not beneficial, the landlord will have to disclaim it. This might be the case if the landlord has allowable losses to offset against the gain or if the net gain for the tax year is less than the annual exempt amount. Where this is the case and no capital gains tax would be payable, it is preferable to disclaim incorporation relief and benefit from the higher base cost of the shares.

An election to disapply the relief must be made by the second anniversary of 31 January following the end of the tax year (so for an incorporation in 2024/25 by 31 January 2028).

Each person has their own entitlement to incorporation relief, and can elect for it not to apply regardless of the action taken by other shareholders.

17.3. Case Study 1 – Transferring Property Business To A Limited Company

Jack has run an unincorporated property business for many years. After looking at the pros and cons, he decides it would be beneficial to operate as a limited company and transfers his property business to the company in exchange for shares. He has three residential properties that he lets out. The original cost and the current market value of the properties are as follows:

Property	Original	Current market value
1	£200,000	£480,000
2	£250,000	£570,000
3	£300,000	£450,000

Jack receives shares (valued at £1.5 million) in exchange.

17.3.1. SDLT

SDLT is payable by reference to the market value of the properties. As the properties are residential properties, the 3% supplement applies.

The residential rates applying (from 23 September onwards) are as follows:

Property value	SDLT rate	SDLT rate with supplement
Up to £250,000	Zero	3%
The next £675,000 (portion from £250,001 to £925,000)	5%	8%
The next £575,000 (portion from £925,000 to £1.5 million)	10%	13%
The remaining amount (above £1.5 million)	12%	15%

If the sale completes on or before 1 June 2024, Jack will benefit from multiple dwellings relief. Where the relief applies, the SDLT payable is calculated by reference to the average value of the property, which in this case is £500,000 (subject to a minimum charge of 1% of the consideration). For each property, the SDLT payable is £27,500 ((£250,000 @ 3%) + (£250,000 @ 8%) a total bill of £82,500 (3 x £27,500).

Multiple dwellings releif is abolished in respect of completions on or after 1 June 2024, unless contracts were exchanged on or before 6 March 2024. From that date, SDLT is calculated by reference to the linked transaction rules and is calculated on the total consideration of £1.5 million. The SDLT payable is therefore £136,250 ((£250,000 @ 3%) + (£675,000 @ 8%) + (£575,000 @ 13%))

The SDLT cost of transferring the properties into the company is significant. The tax savings of incorporation have to outweigh this for incorporation to be worthwhile for Jack. If Jack wishes to go ahead, completing before 1 June 2024 will enable him to reduce the bill by £53,750 by claiming multiple dwellings relief. This is a significant saving.

17.3.2. Capital Gains Tax

On transferring the properties to the limited company, Jack would realise chargeable gains of £650,000. For the sake of simplicity, costs of acquisition and disposal are ignored here, but would be taken into account in reality in computing the gain.

Property	Original	Current market value	Gain
1	£200,000	£480,000	£280,000
2	£250,000	£570,000	£220,000
3	£300,000	£450,000	£150,000

As the conditions for incorporation relief are met, the gain is rolled over and the base cost of the shares is reduced by the gain of £650,000 to £850,000 (£1.5 million - £650,000).

17.3.3. Summary

To incorporate the business Jack will incur an immediate SDLT charge of either £82,500 or £136,250 depending on whether multiple dwellings relief is available (plus the costs of setting up the company). He will trigger a chargeable gain of £650,000 which is rolled over against the cost of the shares and which will crystallise when (or if) the shares are sold.

17.4. New Landlords – Setting Up a Property Limited Company

Where a person is thinking of setting up a property company, operating as a limited company from the get-go avoids the costs of transferring an existing business (and the properties in that business) into the limited company.

The landlord will need to set up a limited company. Advice on how to do this can be found on the Gov.uk website. The company must be registered with Companies House. This can be done using the online service on the Gov.uk website. The company will be registered for corporation tax at the same time.

The new company will need to purchase properties to let and SDLT (or LBTT/LTT as appropriate) will be payable at the residential or commercial rates, depending on the type of property purchased. Where finance is needed, the company will need to borrow the money, rather than the landlord.

17.5. Taxation of Company Profits

The profits of a property company are chargeable to corporation tax.

For the financial year 2023 (starting on 1 April 2023) the rate depends on the level of the company's profits. The rate is set at 19% where profits do not exceed the lower limit, at 25% where profits exceed the upper limit and at the rate of 25% less marginal relief where profits fall between the lower and upper limits. For a standalone company, the lower limit is set at £50,000 and the upper limit at £250,000. If the company has one or more associated companies, the limits are divided by the number of associated companies plus one. . The lower and upper limits are also proportionately reduced for accounting periods of less than 12 months.

Marginal relief is found by the formula:

F x (U-A) x N/A
Where:
- F is the marginal relief fraction (set at 3/200 for the financial year 2023);
- U is the upper limit;
- A is the amount of augmented profits (profits plus dividends from non-group companies); andN is the amount of total taxable profit.

Where N and A are the same, N/A =1 and the formula can be simplified to F x (U – N). Where this is the case, profits are taxed at 19% up to the lower profits limit, at 26.5% between the lower profits limit and the upper profits limit and at 25% on profits in excess of the upper profits limit.

Corporation tax is payable nine months and one day from the end of the accounting period to which it relates.

17.5.1. Accruals Basis

The cash basis does not apply to companies. Consequently, where a business is operated as a property rental business, profits must be computed using the accruals basis in accordance with GAAP. This means that rental income is taken into account for the period to which it relates, rather than when it was received. Likewise expenses are deducted in the period to which they relate, rather than the period in which they are paid. Under the accruals basis, it is necessary to take account of accruals and prepayments and to reflect debtors and creditors.

17.5.2. Deduction For Expenses

Expenses can be deducted in computing profits to the extent that they relate wholly and exclusively to the property business. The types of expenses that can be deducted will include:

- accounting costs;
- administrative expenses;
- advertising for tenants;
- cleaning;
- repairs and maintenance;
- vehicle costs;
- finance costs;
- utilities;
- insurance;

- gardening;
- ground rent.

Records should be kept to ensure that all allowable expenses are taken into account when computing profits.

17.5.3. Deduction For Mortgage Interest And Other Finance Costs

The restriction on tax relief for finance costs that applies to unincorporated property businesses (other than those with furnished holiday lettings for 2024/25 and earlier tax years or commercial property) does not apply to companies, and where finance costs are significant and the landlord is a higher rate taxpayer, one of the main advantages to operating through a limited company is the ability to deduct interest and finance costs in full in computing profits.

When calculating the profits of the company, the allowable finance costs, such as mortgage interest (but not capital repayments) and arrangement fees, are simply deducted from rental income, giving relief at the same rate as that at which profits are charged to corporation tax.

By contrast, an unincorporated landlord cannot deduct finance costs when working out profits of the property rental business. Instead, 20% of the costs are deducted from the tax that is payable (as a tax reduction). The tax reduction is given at the basic rate of 20%, even if the landlord is a higher or additional rate taxpayer and is capped at 20% of the tax due on the rental profits. Unrelieved interest and finance costs can be carried forward to later tax years.

17.6. Taxation Of Capital Gains

Chargeable gains realised by a company are charged to corporation tax, rather than to capital gains tax. The gains are worked out in the same way as for those realised by an individual, but there is no annual exempt amount.

Unlike individuals, all gains realised by a company are taxed at the same rate – the company's effective rate of corporation tax. By contrast, individuals pay capital gains tax at 10% where total income and gains do not exceed the basic rate band (£37,700 for 2023/24) and at 20% once income and gains exceed this level. A higher rate applies to residential property gains, which are taxed at 18% where income and gains do not exceed the basic rate band, and at 24% where they do. Prior to 6 April 2024, the higher capital gains tax rate on residential gains was set at 28%. Individuals benefit from an annual exempt amount for capital gains tax (set at £3,000 for 2024/25). There is no equivalent for companies, meaning companies pay tax on the first £3,000 of net chargeable gains, whereas an individual does not.

Corporation tax on chargeable gains realised by a company are payable as part of the company's corporation tax bill, by the normal due date of nine months and one day from the end of the accounting period. The requirement for individuals to report residential chargeable gains to HMRC within 60 days of completion and to pay a payment on account of the capital gains tax due within the same time frame does not apply to companies, giving companies a significantly longer payment window.

17.7. Extracting Profits From The Company

One of the potential downsides to running a property business through a limited company is the need to extract profits for the personal use of the landlord. This may incur personal tax and National Insurance liabilities on the landlord and, where the profits are extracted as a salary or bonus, the company may also pay National Insurance contributions.

When looking at the overall tax cost of operating through a limited company, it is necessary to take into account not only the tax payable by the company, but also the tax payable by the landlord personally on extracted profits (plus any National Insurance payable by the landlord and the company).

Popular ways of extracting profits are considered below.

17.7.1. Salary

If the landlord has no other income and his or her personal allowance is available, it can be tax efficient to pay a small salary. Paying a salary at least equal to the lower earnings limit for National Insurance purposes (set at £6,396 for 2024/25) will ensure the year is a qualifying year for state pension purposes too. If the landlord already has the 35 qualifying years needed for a full state pension, this will not be a consideration.

For 2024/25, the optimal salary is one equal to the primary threshold of £12,570 as long as the personal allowance remains available to shelter the salary from tax.

As long as the salary does not exceed the available personal allowance, there is no personal income tax to pay.

If the employment allowance is not available, employer's National Insurance at 13.8% will be payable where the salary exceeds the secondary threshold (£175 per week, £758 per month, £9,100 per year for year 2024/25). A higher secondary threshold (equivalent of £50,270 a year) applies where the recipient is under the age of 21, an apprentice under the age of 25 or an armed forced veteran in the first year of their first civilian employment since leaving the armed forces. A higher secondary threshold (equivalent to £25,000 a year) also applies to new employees of employers with physical premises in a special tax site such as a Freeport. The employment allowance is not available to personal company where the sole employee is also a director.

Employee's National Insurance is payable if the salary exceeds the primary threshold (set at £242 per week, £1,048 per month, £12,570 per year for 2024/25) at the rate of 8% on earnings up to the upper earnings limit (£967 per week, £4,189 per month, £50,270 per year) and at 2% thereafter.

It should be remembered that directors have an annual earnings period and the annual thresholds are used to work out their liability.

However, the salary and any associated employer's National Insurance contributions are deductible in computing the company's profits chargeable to corporation tax, so will save corporation tax at the appropriate rate (between 19% and 25%) depending on the company's profits.

17.7.2. Dividends

Once a salary up to the optimal level has been taken, it is tax efficient to extract further profits as dividends, rather than to pay a higher salary or a bonus.

However, there are strict rules governing the payment of dividends. Dividends can only be paid out of retained profits, so if the company wishes to pay a dividend, it must have sufficient retained profits from which to pay it. Dividends must also be paid in proportion to shareholdings; thus where there is more than one shareholder, having an alphabet share structure can be beneficial to allow dividends to be tailored to the circumstances of the recipient.

As dividends are paid out of post-tax profits, the funds from which they are paid have already suffered corporation tax. This will be at the rate of between 19% and 25% from 1 April 2023 onwards. Depending on the level of dividends paid, there may be further tax to pay by the shareholder.

All taxpayer's regardless of the rate at which they pay tax are entitled to a dividend allowance, set at £500 for 2024/25. Dividends covered by the allowance are taxed at a zero rate. If the shareholder has not used their personal allowance in full, there will also be no further tax to pay on dividends to the extent that they are sheltered by the personal allowance. Once all the available allowances have been used up, dividends (which are treated as the top slice of income) are for 2024/25 taxed at 8.75%% to the extent that they fall within the basic rate band, 33.75% to the extent that they fall within the higher rate band and 39.35% to the extent that they fall within the additional rate band.

17.7.3. Other Ways Of Extracting Funds From The Company

Paying a salary and taking dividends are not the only routes by which profits can be taken out of the company for the landlord's personal use.

If the company is run from the landlord's home, the company can rent the home office space. The landlord will be taxable on the rental income while the company can deduct the rental income in computing profits. However, it should be noted that the property income allowance is not available in this situation.

The company can also provide benefits in kind. Where the benefit is exempt from tax and National Insurance, this can be tax efficient as there is no tax liability or Class 1A National Insurance, and the company can deduct the cost of providing the benefit when computing their profits.

The company can also make pension contributions on the landlord's behalf (as long as there is a sufficient annual allowance available). This too can be tax efficient as the company can deduct the cost of the pension contributions when calculating their profits.

17.7.4. Leave Profits In The Company

Once the landlord has extracted profits needed for personal use and the extraction of further profits will trigger tax liabilities, if they are not needed outside the company, it is more tax efficient to leave them in the company, and to take out later when this can be done at a lower tax cost.

17.8. Annual Tax On Enveloped Dwellings (ATED)

Where residential property valued at more than £500,000 is held in a company, the annual tax on enveloped dwellings (ATED) must be considered. Relief is available for qualifying rental businesses.

17.8.1. Nature Of The ATED

The ATED is payable where high value residential property is held within an 'envelope', such as a limited company. The charge applies if a dwelling in the UK that is valued at more than £500,000 is owned, or partly owned, by:

- a company;
- a partnership where at least one of the partners is a company; or
- a collective investment scheme, such as a unit trust or an open-ended investment vehicle.

A number of exemptions and relief are available. Of particular relevance is the one for qualifying property rental businesses.

17.8.2. Relief For Qualifying Property Rental Businesses

Relief from ATED is available where there is a qualifying rental business. To qualify:

- the business must be a property rental business; and
- it must be carried out on a commercial basis with a view to profit.

The property must be let to a third party, and not occupied by an owner.

If the company is not currently generating receipts, all is not lost – relief remains available if steps are being taken to use the property to generate an income without delay, such as advertising for a tenant.

Relief, however, is not available if the property is held in a company which is not a qualifying property rental business (for example, a trading company), even if it is let commercially.

Where relief is available, a Relief Declaration Return should be submitted instead. This can be done using the ATED Online Service.

17.8.3. Amount Of Charge

Where relief or an exemption is not available, an annual charge applies based on the value of the property at the relevant valuation date. For the 2024/25 chargeable period , the charges are as follows:

Value of property	Annual charge
More than £500,000 up to £1 million	£4,400
More than £1 million up to £2 million	£9,000
More than £2 million up to £5 million	£30,550
More than £5 million up to £10 million	£71,500
More than £10 million up to £20 million	£143,550

| More than £20 million | £287,500 |

The 2024/25 charge period runs from 1 April 2024 to 31 March 2025. Where a property within the charge to ATED is held on 1 April 2024, a return must be filed and the tax must be paid by 30 April 2024. Where a property is acquired after that date, the tax is payable within 30 days of the date on which the property came within the charge to ATED.

For the 2024/25 period, the charge is based on the value at 1 April 2022 (or, if later, the date on which the property was acquired).

17.9. Property Management Companies

A landlord with a private portfolio can set up a property management company to manage their private portfolio. This can be a useful halfway house where the landlord has an existing property portfolio and the costs of transferring it to a limited company would be too high. In this way, some of the profits are charged to corporation tax rather than to income tax. This can be beneficial where the landlord pays income tax at the higher or the additional rate.

The property management company acts as the letting agent and charges the landlord for finding tenants and managing the lets. The property management company would typically undertake any repairs and maintenance that need doing on the properties. These costs would be re-billed to the landlord.

The management company charges the landlord a fee for their services, typically a percentage of the rental income. It is important that this is set at a commercial rate to avoid scrutiny from HMRC. The landlord is able to deduct the fee in calculating the profits of their unincorporated property business.

The property management company pays corporation tax on its profits, currently between 19% and 25% depending on the level of its profits.

Using a property management company can reduce the overall tax bill by moving some profits from the charge to income tax to the charge to corporation tax, which is payable at a lower rate.

It is important that there are commercial reasons for setting up a property management company to avoid challenges from HMRC that it is a tax avoidance arrangement designed solely to save tax.

17.10. Property Limited Company V Unincorporated Property Business

The following case studies compare the tax and National Insurance payable by a landlord operating as a limited company with that payable by a landlord operating as an unincorporated property business.

17.10.1. Case Study 2 – Landlord Is A Basic Rate Taxpayer

Betsy lets out 4 properties, generating rental income of £40,000. She has no other income. She pays mortgage interest of £10,000 a year and incurs other deductible expenses of £5,000.

17.10.2. Unincorporated Property Business

Betsy's tax position for 2024/25 is as follows:

	£
Rental income	40,000
Less: expenses	(5,000)
Profit	35,000
Less: personal allowance	(12,570)
Taxable income	22,430
Tax @ 20%	4,486
Less: income tax reduction (£10,000 @ 20%)	(2,000)
Tax payable	2,486

Betsy pays tax of £2,486.

After tax and expenses, Betsy retains £22,514 of her rental income (£40,000 - £5,000 - £10,000 - £2,486).

17.10.3. Property Company

If Betsy operated her property through a limited company, the company's tax position would be as follows:

	£
Rental income	40,000
Less: expenses	(5,000)
interest	(10,000)
Profit before tax	25,000
Corporation tax @19%	4,750
Profit after tax	20,250

The company retains £20,250 of the rental income. However, Betsy would need to extract the profits if she wanted them for her personal use, which would trigger additional tax liabilities, reducing the net amount available to her.

17.10.4. Comments

In this situation, Betsy is better operating as an unincorporated business. The availability of the personal allowance outweighs the lower rate of corporation tax.

17.11. Case Study 3 – Landlord Is A Higher Rate Taxpayer

Bertie also lets out 4 properties, generating rental income of £40,000. He pays mortgage interest of £10,000 a year and incurs other deductible expenses of £5,000. He has other income of £60,000 and his personal allowance has been utilised against his other income.

17.11.1. Unincorporated Property Business

Bertie's tax position for 2024/25 is as follows:

	£
Rental income	40,000
Less: expenses	(5,000)
Profit	35,000
Tax @ 40%	14,000
Less: income tax reduction (£10,000 @ 20%)	(2,000)
Tax payable	12,000

Bertie will pay tax of £12,000 on his rental income if he operates as an unincorporated property business, leaving £13,000 (£40,000 - £5,000 - £10,000 - £12,000) available for his personal use.

17.11.2. Property Company: Low Profits

If Bertie operated his property through a limited company, the company's tax position would be as for Betsy above, as follows:

	£
Rental income	40,000
Less: expenses	(5,000)
interest	(10,000)
Profit before tax	25,000
Corporation tax @19%	4,750
Profit after tax	20,250

The company retains £20,250 of the rental income. This is significantly higher than that retained by Bertie's unincorporated property business. However, this is not the end of the story as if Bertie wishes to have the profits available for his personal use, he must extract them from the company.

As he has already used up his personal allowance, it will be more tax efficient to take the profits as dividends. Bertie has not used his dividend allowance elsewhere.
If he extracts all the profits as a dividend, the tax payable on the dividend is as follows:

	£
Dividend	20,250
Less: dividend allowance	(500))
Taxable dividend	19,750
Tax @ 33.75%	(6,665.63)
Retained by Bertie	13,584.37

If Bertie extracts all the profits as dividends, the amount retained by him is less than if he operates as an unincorporated property business.

However, the tax paid by the company is considerably less than that paid by Bertie's unincorporated property business. If he does not need to extract the profits and can leave them in the company to extract at a future date, operating as a limited company will be a more tax-efficient option. However, if he needs all the profits for his personal use, the tax hit on the dividend at the higher dividend rate of 33.75%% (in addition to the corporation tax already paid on the profits) means that the pendulum swings the other way, and he will retain more of his rental income if he operates as an unincorporated business.

17.11.3. Case Study 5: Company Benefits from Marginal Relief

Bella has a property limited company which has taxable rental profits of £100,000 for the year to 31 March 2024. The company has no interest and finance costs.

The company will pay benefit from marginal relief of £2,250 (3/200 x (£250,000 - £100,000)) and will pay corporation tax of £22,750 ((£100,000 @ 25%) - £2,250) – an effective rate of 22.75%. This leaves the company with after tax profits of £77,250.
If Bella extracts the profits as a dividend, assuming she has no other income, she will pay tax of £12,360.75 ((£12,570 @ 0%) + (£500 @ 0%) = (£37,200 @ 8.75%) + (£26,980 @ 33.75%)). She will retain ££64,889 of the rental profits.

Had Bella operated as an unincorporated landlord with rental profits of £100,000, she would have paid tax of £27,430, leaving her with £72,568 of the rental profits. She is therefore better operating as an unincorporated business, as although the corporation tax bill is less than the income tax bill, if she wishes to use the profits outside the company, she will also pay tax on the dividends.

17.11.4. Case Study 5: High Profits

Bill has a property company and has rental profits of £300,000 for the year to 31 March 2024. The company has no interest and finance costs. It will pay corporation tax on those profits at 25%, a bill of £75,000, leaving post tax profits of £225,000 available to extract for Bill's personal use.

If he extracts all the profits as a dividend, he will pay tax on that dividend of £72,060,91 ((£500 @ 0%) + (£37,200 @ 8.75%) + (87,440 @ 33.75%) + (£99,860 @ 39.35%)), leaving him with post tax profits of £152,939.

Had Bill operated as an unincorporated landlord, he would have paid income tax of £121,203 ((£37,700 @ 20%) + (£87,440 @ 40%) + (£174,860 @ 45%)). This will leave him with £178,797 after tax. Again this is more than if he had operated as a company and extracted all the profits as dividends.

As Bill's income exceeds £125,140, he has lost all of his personal allowance.

17.11.5. Final Thoughts

As has been demonstrated above, there are advantaged and disadvantages of operating as a limited company. Each landlord will need to assess their own personal circumstances.

The decision as to whether it is better to operate as a limited company or as an unincorporated property rental business will depend on the rate at which the company pays corporation tax, the rate at which the landlord pays tax, whether his or her personal allowance has been used elsewhere and whether they need to extract profits from the company for personal use. There is no substitute for crunching the numbers.

Stamp Duty Land & Property Tax

18. Saving On Stamp Duty

In this section you will understand when you are liable to pay stamp duty.

18.1. When Do Property Investors Pay Stamp Duty?

The following table provides details of the current rates of stamp duty for residential property which have become effective from 23 September 2022.

A new series of stamp duty rates have been introduced for second and subsequent residential properties, which will be effective for property investors.

Stamp Duty Rates

	First residential property	Second and subsequent residential properties – from 1 April 2016
When payment for the property is up to £40,000	Zero	Zero
When payment for the property is over £40,000, then the SDLT on any amount up to the first £250,000	Zero	3%
Next £675,000 (£250,001 to £925,000)	5%	8%
Next £575,000 (£925,001 to £1.5 million)	10%	13%
Remainder above £1.5m	12%	15%

The example that follows will assume that the second and subsequent residential properties stamp duty rate applies.

18.1.1. Stamp Duty When Buying New Land Or Property

When purchasing land or property, you will be liable to pay stamp duty before you have completed the deal. Typically, the solicitor acting on your behalf in the transaction will include this tax liability in his final invoice to you.

Stamp Duty Land Tax When Purchasing A Second Property

Howard buys a buy-to-let property for £500,000.

> The rates of stamp duty will be as follows:
>
> The first £250,000   -   3%
> The next £250,000   -   8%
>
> The means the total amount payable will be:
>
> The first £250,000   -   £7,50 (£250,000 * 0.03)
> The next £250,000   -   £20,000 (£250,000 * 0.08)
>
> Total Due: £27,500
>
> This means the total amount of stamp duty due is £27,500.

18.1.2. Stamp Duty When Transferring A Property

What a lot of investors fail to realise is that if you transfer ownership of a property to another party (including husband/wife), then stamp duty will be liable if the property is mortgaged and the mortgage amount being transferred is over the relevant SDLT threshold. The 3% supplement does not apply where the transfer is between spouses or civil partners as long as no one else is involved in the transaction.

If the property is not mortgaged and ownership is being gifted, then there is no stamp duty liability.

Other Property Investment Strategies

19. Tax-Free Income For Renting Out Part Of Your Home

In this section you will learn about generous annual tax-free savings that are available if you rent out part of your main home.

This tax relief is known as the **rent-a-room** relief.

19.1. What Is The Rent-A-Room Relief?

If you decide to let a room in your main residence, you can receive a rental income of up to £7,500 and have no tax liability[1]

In order to claim this allowance, the property must satisfy the following conditions:

a) you must also live in the property as your main home, at the same time as the tenant, for at least part of the letting period in each tax year;

b) the room you are letting out must be fully furnished.

If you claim the rent-a-room relief, then it is not possible to claim any expenditure that you have incurred with regards to the letting.

This is a very common strategy for those people who have houses that are too large for their needs. For example, if your children have left home, then you may decide to rent the room they lived in for an additional tax-free income.

> **Rent-a-Room Relief (1)**
>
> Bill and Mary have a three-bedroom detached house. They are both higher-rate taxpayers.
>
> Their daughter Louise leaves home and moves in with her long-term boyfriend, so they decide to let her room out to a local teacher.
>
> They receive an annual rental income of £4,000 per annum.
>
> There is no tax liability on this income as it is below the £7,500 threshold value.

If the income received is greater than the annual allowance, then tax is liable on the amount above this value.

---

[1] All that is necessary is to tick the rent-a-room box at the beginning of the land and property page of the tax return.

> **Rent-a-Room Relief (2)**
>
> Howard is a bachelor but lives in a luxury five-bedroom detached house on the outskirts of London. He is also a higher-rate taxpayer.
>
> He decides to let a room to a newly graduated doctor for £8,500 per annum.
>
> Howard will have no tax liability on the first £7,500. However, he will be liable to pay tax on the remaining £1,000 of income at 40%. This means that he will be liable to pay £400 in tax.

If you decide to let a room in your main residence and claim the relief, then you must inform HMRC. This is regardless of whether you will have a tax liability.

If you do not inform HMRC, then you will be taxed as though you are running a normal property-letting business, where your expenses will be deducted from any rental income you receive.

19.2. Choosing Not to Use The Relief

> Consider not using the relief if you have high income and also high expenses.

If you are letting a room in your property, then it is not necessary that you claim the relief. As mentioned in the previous section, you will be taxed as a normal property-letting business if you do not inform HMRC that you want to use the relief.

Generally speaking, if your rental income is going to be significantly greater than £7,500, then it may not be beneficial to use the relief.

The following two case studies illustrate typical scenarios when it is beneficial to use each method.

> **When it is Beneficial to Use the Rent-a-Room Relief**
>
> John is a higher-rate taxpayer and lets out a room in his property for £10,000 per annum. His expenses are £1,000.
>
> Tax liability if rent-a-room relief is *not* claimed
> If rent-a-room relief is not claimed, then he has a taxable income of £9,000 (i.e., £10,000 – £1,000).
>
> This means that his tax liability is calculated as follows:
> 40% × £9,000 = **£3,600**
>
> Tax liability if rent-a-room relief *is* claimed

> If rent-a-room relief is claimed, then he has a taxable income of £2,500 (i.e., £10,000 – £7,500).
>
> This means that his tax liability is calculated as follows:
> 40% × £2,500 = **£1,000**

As you can see from the above case study, it is beneficial for John to claim the rent-a-room relief. This is because by claiming it, John will pay **£2,600** less in tax on an annual basis. Over a 10-year period, this is **£26,000** in tax savings.

> **When it is NOT Beneficial to Use the Rent-a-Room Relief**
>
> Lisa is a higher-rate taxpayer and lets out a room in her property for £13,000 per annum. Her expenses are £9,000 per annum.
>
> Tax liability if rent-a-room relief is *not* claimed
> If rent-a-room relief is not claimed, then she has a taxable income of £4,000 (i.e., £13,000 – £9,000).
>
> This means that her tax liability is calculated as follows:
> 40% × £4,000 = **£1,600**
>
> Tax liability if rent-a-room relief *is* claimed
> If rent-a-room relief is claimed, then she has a taxable income of £4,500 (i.e., £13,000 – £7,500).
>
> This means that her tax liability is calculated as follows:
> 40% × £5,500 = **£2,200**

As you can see from the above case study, it is beneficial for Lisa *not* to use the rent-a-room relief. This is because by claiming it, Lisa will pay **£600** less in tax on an annual basis. Over a 10-year period, this is **£6,000** in tax savings.

> It is possible to switch between the 'Rent-a-Room' allowance and the "strict" method from year to year if you wish.

19.3. Renting Out In Joint Ownership

The exemption limit of £7,500 is reduced to £3,750 if during the tax year to April 5, someone else received income from letting accommodation in the same property.

This is likely to occur if you own a property in a partnership.

20. Generous Tax Breaks For Holiday Lets

In this section you will become familiar with the tax benefits associated with those who provide holiday lets.

20.1. Qualifying Criteria For A Holiday Let

If you let a property in a popular holiday location, e.g., the south coast, then you could well be operating a holiday lettings business. This is especially the case if your target market is people visiting and staying in your property for short periods of time.

In order to qualify your property as a holiday let, it must be fully furnished; that is, anyone moving into the property must be able to live out of the property without having to buy any additional furniture/furnishings.

It must also satisfy the following three conditions:

- the property must be available to let to the public on a commercial basis for at least 210 days;
- the property must be let for at least 105 days;
- let for periods of longer-term occupation (more than 31 consecutive days) for not more than 155 days during the year.

Income tax on a holiday let is charged in the same way as if you are operating a normal lettings business, where tax will be liable on any rental profits less expenses.

> **Holiday Lets**
>
> John buys a three-bedroom property in Bournemouth. His investment strategy is to rent the property in the summer periods to visiting holiday makers.
>
> He offers the property for £250 per week.
>
> Over the financial year, it is let for 35 weeks, which means that he has received a total rental income of £8,750. His expenses are £2,750.
>
> This means that he is liable to pay tax on the £6,000 profit.

20.2. Three Generous Tax Benefits Associated With Holiday Lets

Operating a holiday letting business has three *significant* tax benefits. These are detailed below.

20.2.1. Interest Relief

The rules restricting interest relief for residential landlords do not apply to FHL's.

20.2.2. Re-investment Of Capital Gains

If you decide to sell your holiday let and make a capital gain, then the sale proceeds can be re-invested into another qualifying asset, thus avoiding any immediate capital gains tax liability. This therefore means that you will not be liable to pay any capital gains tax until you dispose of the asset you have re-invested in.

However, you can continue selling and re-investing the sale proceeds. By doing this, you will continue to defer any tax liability until the point at which you stop re-investing the sales proceeds.

> **Holiday Lets – Re-investment of Capital Gains**
>
> Karen buys a property for £130,000 which she lets out as a holiday let. She sells her property 5 years later for £230,000, thus meaning she has made a profit of £100,000.
>
> She buys another 'holiday let' property in the same tax year by re-investing the sale proceeds and therefore is able to defer any CGT liability.

20.2.3. Relevant Earnings

FHL earnings count as relevant earnings with respect to pension contribution rules.

Please note, the special tax regime for furnished holiday lettings is to be abolished from 6 April 2025.

21. Tax Tips For Landlords Renovating Properties

A renovation project can be very appealing. Buying a property that needs work can be cost effective and financially worthwhile, particularly if the property can be secured for a good price. Doing the property up will add value, and the hope is that it will provide the opportunity to realise a sizeable gain. Renovating a property, either to live in, sell on or to rent out, allows for the possibility of turning a property that needs work into a desirable residence.

A landlord may also take advantage of an empty period to do up a buy-to-let property or a property let as a furnished holiday let.

When doing up a property, the tax implications should be considered at the outset. Not all renovation routes are equal, and the tax costs can greatly affect the overall financial outcomes achieved.

21.1. Investment Vs Trading

Trading profits are taxed to income tax or corporation tax, depending on whether or not the business is operated as a company. By contrast, a gain that is realised on an investment property is charged to capital gains tax where the gain is realised by an individual or to corporation tax where the gain is realised by a company. The rates of income tax, corporation tax and capital gains tax differ and it is important to understand at the start of the project how any eventual profit or gain may be taxed.

21.1.1. Investment Properties

As a general rule, a property will be treated as having been purchased as an investment if the intention is to keep it for some time, either as an income-earning asset or in order to benefit from long-term capital growth. This may be the case where a property is purchased as a renovation project with a view to letting it out as a buy-to-let or as furnished holiday accommodation once it has been renovated. The intention at the outset is key here.

Where the property is sold, if it is owned by one or more individuals, any chargeable gain arising on the sale is liable to capital gains tax. If the property is held in a company, any gain on the sale is charged to corporation tax on capital gains.

21.1.2. Trading

Where the intention is to do the property up and sell it quickly for a profit, the property is likely to be treated as trading stock rather than as an investment property. A property developer who buys a property, renovates it and immediately sells it, moving on to the next project straight away is likely to be trading. Any gain on the sale of the renovated property is trading income, charged to income tax or corporation tax as appropriate. Again, intention at the outset is key.

21.1.3. Property Purchased As A Residence

Living in a property as a main residence while renovating it can be attractive, opening the door to the availability of main residence relief for any period where the property is the owner's only or main residence, plus the final nine months of ownership. However, it should be noted that anti-avoidance legislation exists which can deny the availability of the main residence exemption where the property is purchased with the intention of making a gain. However, in practice this can be difficult to prove.

21.1.4. The Impact Of Intention

As noted above, the tax treatment of any gain realised on a renovation project will depend on whether the property is an investment property, whether the purchaser is trading or whether the property is lived in as a main residence. Here intention is key.

Circumstances change and it is not possible to know what may happen in the future. As a result, plans may need to be revised as circumstances change. A property may be purchased as an investment property, with a view to letting once renovated for the foreseeable future, but a change in circumstance may force a sale to release funds.

A change of circumstance does not turn an investment project into a property trade, but without evidence of the initial intention, it may be difficult to resist any contention from HMRC that the profit on sale is a trading profit chargeable to income tax rather than a chargeable gain. Where the business is operated through a company, this is less of an issue as both trading profits and chargeable gains are liable to corporation tax. However, for an individual, particularly where income tax is payable at the higher or additional rates, the additional tax hit could be sizeable.

It is therefore good practice to keep documentary evidence to back up the original intention when purchasing the property. This may include:

- Financial projections to show the projected outcome for the project, whether in making a short-term gain or in securing rental income over the longer term.
- Emails and other correspondence, for example, with letting agents investigating potential rental yield and amounts charged by letting agents for their services.
- Personal correspondence that supports the contention that the property was being purchased as a home.

21.2. Buying The Renovation Property: SDLT

Having found the right property to renovate, the first tax liability to arise is likely to be Stamp Duty Land Tax (SDLT) where the property is in England or Northern Ireland. Land and Buildings Transaction Tax (LBTT) applies to properties in Scotland and Land Transaction Tax (LTT) applies to properties in Wales.

21.3. Relief For The Costs of Doing Up The Property

The extent to which tax relief is availablef for the costs of doing up the property will depend on whether the project is a property development project or an investment project, or whether a person is simply renovating their own home.

The focus here is on development and investment properties. There is no relief for revenue expenditure incurred while renovating your home. However, relief for capital expenditure on improving the property will be taken into account in computing any chargeable gain that arises when the property is sold in the event that the property has not been the taxpayer's only or main residence throughout.

21.3.1. Revenue V Capital Expenditure

When renovating the property, the expenditure incurred will either be revenue in nature or capital in nature. This is an important distinction as it affects how relief, if any, is given for the expense.

In deciding which camp an expense falls, the key question is whether the expense is incurred to repair or restore the property to its previous condition or whether it will enhance or improve the property. The former is likely to be a revenue expense and the latter a capital expense.

21.3.2. Repairs – Relief For Revenue Expenses

As a general rule, a deduction is available when computing profits for revenue expenses to the extent that they are incurred wholly and exclusively for the purposes of the business. This is the case regardless of whether the accounts are prepared using the accruals basis or the cash basis.

However, this is only relevant where there are taxable profits to be calculated, either because a property developer is trading or there is an on-going rental business. If the property being renovated is to be used as a second home once it has been done up and sold at some future date, there are no taxable profits to calculate and nothing to set any revenue expenses against. The same is true where a main home is renovated. However, if the intention is to renovate a property prior to letting it, some relief may be available under the rules for pre-letting expenditure.

Where repairs are undertaken by a property developer, the costs will be deductible in working out trading profits. Likewise, where there is an on-going property business, the cost of any repairs or maintenance which is undertaken can be deducted in working out the profit of the property income business.

All properties need maintaining and a landlord will need a budget for repairs and maintenance. Expenses that fall into this category will include repairs to a roof or a fence, repainting and decorating, repairing doors and windows, treating damp and rot and such like. Sometimes it will be necessary to replace an item where it cannot be repaired, for example, where windows are rotten. A replacement will count as a revenue item where it is a like-for-like replacement. HMRC have also confirmed that the cost of an upgraded new boiler is allowable as a revenue expense where the upgrade is due to an advance in technology and the upgraded boiler does broadly the same job as the old boiler. However, if the replacement expenditure enhances the property beyond that resulting simply from using newer materials, it will be improvement expenditure, which is capital.

21.3.3. Capital Expenditure

Expenditure on acquiring the land and property itself is capital expenditure, as is anything which enhances or improves the property, such as building an extension or significantly upgrading the property, for example, replacing a wall and an old single door with bi-fold doors, upgrading the kitchen and the bathroom, etc. The question to ask is whether as a result of the expenditure the property has been significantly improved.

Where a renovation project is undertaken, there is likely to be a significant degree of improvement, and much of the expenditure is likely to be capital in nature, rather than revenue expenditure. However, it should be noted that where the degree of improvement is so small as to be incidental to a repair, the expenditure remains revenue expenditure. This is also the case where any improvement is simply down to improvements in the materials available or technological advances. This may be the case where an old building is repaired using modern materials or old single-glazed windows are replaced with double glazing.

21.3.4. Extensive Alterations To The Property

The work undertaken in a renovation project may be significant. Where alterations to a property are so significant as to amount to a reconstruction of the property, HMRC regard the expenditure as being capital in nature. Consequently, no deduction is allowed for expenses that would normally be treated as revenue expenses. The exception to this is the cost of any repairs to any part of the old building, which is preserved, which are deductible in the usual way.

21.3.5. Repairs To A Dilapidated Property – The Capital Expenditure Trap

When buying a property, the price of the property will reflect the state that the property is in. A property that is in a dilapidated state will generally be cheaper than one that is a good state. The fact that repairs are undertaken shortly after a property has been acquired will not in itself mean that the expenditure is capital rather than revenue. However, depending on the circumstances, HMRC may take the view that the expenditure on the necessary repairs is capital rather than revenue. Watch points to look out for include:

- a property which when acquired was not in a fit state to use until repairs had been carried out, or which could not be let until repairs had been undertaken;
- the price paid for the property being substantially reduced because of its dilapidated state.

Under these circumstances, repairs costs may be treated as capital expenditure. However, where the price of the property simply reflects normal wear and tear (such as outdated decoration), repair costs, even if undertaken shortly after acquisition, remain revenue expenditure.

21.3.6. Splitting Expenditure Between Capital and Revenue

When renovating a property, work may be commissioned which incorporates both improvement work and repair work to be undertaken at the same time. Any expenditure on repairs remains allowable and can be deducted in the usual way. The split between the capital expenditure and the repairs may be apparent from the contractor's bill or invoice. Where the contractor does not provide a breakdown, the costs can be apportioned in a just and reasonable fashion.

21.3.7. Relief For Capital Expenditure – Cash Basis

Where accounts are prepared using the cash basis, a deduction is permitted for capital expenditure in calculating profits, for example, those of an on-going property business, unless the capital expenditure is of a type for which a deduction is expressly excluded.

The main exclusions are expenditure on acquiring, altering or disposing of the land. The prohibition does not apply to expenditure on an asset which is fixed to the qualifying land so to become part of that land, unless the asset in question is one of the following:

- a building;
- a wall, floor, ceiling, door, gate, shutter, window or stairs;
- a waste disposal system;
- sewerage or drainage system;
- a shaft or other structure in which a lift, hoist, escalator or moving walkway may be installed.

Thus, even where the cash basis is used, items on the above list cannot be deducted in calculating taxable profits. Relief may be available in the form of capital allowances, although the scope to claim capital allowances for a property rental business is limited.

A deduction is also denied for expenditure on an item of a capital nature incurred on, or in connection with, the provision, alteration or disposal of any asset that is not acquired or created for use on a continuing basis in the property business.

Also excluded is expenditure on the provision, alteration or disposal of an assets used in an ordinary residential rental property (for which relief is given under the replacement of domestic items rules). Here, an ordinary residential property is a residential property in respect of which a property rental business is carried on, but which for 2024/25 and earlier tax years excludes furnished holiday lettings. Thus, when renovating a property, enhancement and improvement expenditure cannot be deducted in calculating profits even where the cash basis is used.

21.3.8. Relief For Capital Expenditure – Accruals Basis

Under the accruals basis, only revenue expenditure can be deducted in calculating profits. Capital allowances may be available for some items of capital expenditure, but in a letting context this is limited, although more generous rules apply to furnished holiday lettings under the tax rules that apply to furnished holiday lettings for 2024/25 and previous tax years.

21.3.9. Relief For Capital Expenditure – Capital Gains

Improvement or enhancement expenditure is taken into account and added to the cost of the asset when working out any gain on disposal which may be chargeable to capital gains or, where the business is operated through a company, corporation tax on chargeable gains.

Where the renovation project involves doing up a second home, relief for the capital costs will be given in working out the gain on the eventual sale.

21.3.10. Relief For Pre-Letting Expenditure

It may be the case that a landlord purchases a property to renovate and then let out. While the renovation work is going on, the property is not available for letting and does not form part of a property rental business. Therefore, there is no rental income and no profits to calculate, so no deduction can be given at that time.

However, all is not lost. The tax rules recognise that it may be necessary to incur expenses prior to letting so that the property can be let out. Relief is available for expenses incurred before the property is first let where the expenditure:

- is incurred within a period of seven years before the date on which the property rental business started;
- is not otherwise allowable; and
- would have been deductible if the expenses were incurred after the property rental business had commenced.

21.3.11. Work Undertaken While Rental Property Is Empty

A landlord may decide to undertake repairs or improvements to an existing rental property, either because these are needed or to enhance the property with a view to increasing the rental yield. The property will not be available for letting while the work is carried out. However, where there is a temporary break in letting to enable repairs or alterations to be undertaken, HMRC will normally accept that the property rental business is on-going. Consequently, expenses will be deductible in accordance with normal rules. Relief will also be due if the landlord undertakes the work between tenants. This may include re-decorating the property or replacing the carpets.

21.4. VAT

If you are using a contractor who is registered for VAT, you may be able to benefit from a 5% rate of VAT on goods and services supplied in connection with the renovation if the property is a dwelling that has not been lived in for two years and, once renovated, it is intended for use as a residential property.

To benefit, you may need to convince your contractor that the reduced rate applies. You can refer them to VAT Notice 708 which contains the detail. However, if your contractor charges you VAT at 20%, you cannot reclaim the difference between this and the reduced rate of 5%, even if you think you are eligible for the reduced rate. It is therefore important to have the conversation with the contractor up front.

21.5. Selling The Property

21.5.1. Selling An Investment Property

Where the property is an investment property, any gain arising on disposal is chargeable to capital gains tax. Any capital costs incurred in doing up a residential property will be taken into account in working out the chargeable gain, which after allowing for any allowable losses and available annual exemptions, is chargeable at the residential property rates. For 2024/25, these are 18% to the extent to which total taxable income and gains do not exceed the basic rate band of £37,700, and 24% once the basic rate band has been used. The annual exempt amount is set at £3,000 for 2024/25.

Residential property gains must be reported to HMRC within 60 days of completion, and tax on account of the capital gains tax due must be paid within the same time frame.

If the property is held in a limited company, the gain is liable to corporation tax on chargeable gains and payable as part of the company's corporation tax bill. Unlike capital gains tax, there is no need to report the gain and pay the tax within 60 days of completion.

21.5.2. Property Development – Taxing the Profit On Sale

Where the renovation constitutes a property development – undertaken with the intention of realising a profit – the profit on sale will be treated a trading profit and taxed to income tax or corporation tax as appropriate.

21.5.3. Selling The Main Residence

If the property which is renovated is the owner's main home and was lived in as such while the work was undertaken, any gain on sale will be covered by the main residence exemption and free of capital gains tax. If the property is purchased and renovated with the sole aim of making a gain, HMRC may challenge the availability of the main residence exemption. It important, therefore, to provide retain evidence that the property was in fact purchased with the intention of being a home.

If the property was lived in as a main home while undertaking the renovation work and subsequently let, any gain on disposal will be sheltered by the main residence exemption to the extent the property was occupied as an only or main residence, plus the last nine months (or, where the owner leaves the property to go into care, the last 36 months). The gain is time apportioned.

21.6. Converting A Property Into Flats - Case Studies

Many a property developer has spotted the potential of buying a large property and converting it into flats in order to maximise profit. However, converting a property into flats for financial gain is not the sole preserve of the property developer.

A landlord may decide to convert a property into flats to maximise both rental income in the short term and profit on sale in the longer term. Likewise, a person may decide to convert a former family home into flats to realise the maximum possible gain on disposal. However, as is often the case, the tax implications will vary depending on the circumstances.

The following case studies illustrate the tax considerations that may arise in different circumstances when converting a property into flats.

21.6.1. Case Study 1 – House Converted By A Developer Into Flats For Sale

A developer buys up a large house in a poor state of repair for £400,000. He spends a further £200,000 converting into four flats. The work takes six months. Once complete, the flats are sold for £250,000 each.

The nature of a property developer's trade is to develop properties for profit. As in this scenario the motive is to make a profit rather than to buy the property as an investment, any profit on sale is charged to income tax as a trading profit rather than to capital gains tax. The trading profit would be computed according to normal rules and the profit on this development (£400,000) would be taken into account in computing the developer's trading profits for the period in question.

As the developer is trading, capital gains tax is not in point. Consequently, there is no capital gains tax to pay when the flats are sold.

21.6.2. Case Study 2 – Landlord Converts Rental Property To Flats For Let

A landlord has a number of properties that he lets out. He has owned a large property for a number of years which has been let out as a single dwelling. He decides to convert the property into flats. He then lets the flats for a further couple of years before selling them.

The landlord will be subject to capital gains on any gain made from the sale of the flats. As the flats have always been let and have never been the landlord's main residence, neither main residence relief nor letting relief are in point.

For the purposes of illustration, it is assumed that the landlord originally bought the house in 2007 for £300,000 and let it as a single unit until June 2021, when he converted the property into three flats. The conversion costs were £150,000. Each flat has two bedrooms and is approximately the same size.

The work was completed in November 2021 and the flats were again let until April 2024, when they were put on the market. Flat 1 sold in May 2024 for £220,000, Flat 2 sold in June 2024 for £230,000, and Flat 3 sold in June 2024 for £215,000. It is assumed that in each case the costs of sale are £2,000.

The gains on disposal are as follows:

Flat 1

Proceeds		£220,000
Less: cost of original property (1/3 x £300,000)	£100,000	
Conversion costs (1/3 x £150,000)	£50,000	
		(£150,000)
		£70,000
Less: costs of disposal		(£2,000)
Gain on sale		£68,000

Flat 2

Proceeds		£230,000
Less: cost of original property (1/3 x £300,000)	£100,000	
Conversion costs (1/3 x £150,000)	£50,000	
		(£150,000)
		£80,000

Less: costs of disposal		(£2,000)
Gain on sale		£78,000

Flat 3

Proceeds		£215,000
Less: cost of original property (1/3 x £300,000)	£100,000	
Conversion costs (1/3 x £150,000)	£50,000	
		(£150,000)
		£65,000
Less: costs of disposal		(£2,000)
Gain on sale		£63,000

In each case, the gain on sale must be reported to HMRC within 60 days of completion of the sale. If the landlord's annual exempt amount has not been otherwise used, it can be taken into account when working out the tax that need to be paid on the gain on the sale of the first flat. A payment on account of capital gains tax due on each sale must be made within 60 days of completion.

The landlord's overall capital gains tax position will be finalised on the submission of his 2024/25 tax return, which is due by 31 January 2026.

21.6.3. Case Study 3 – Homeowner Converts House To Flats Prior To Sale

After his children have grown up, a homeowner decides to convert his property into flats prior to sale to maximise the profit on sale. The flats are sold as soon as the work is complete.

For the purposes of illustration, it is assumed that the property was purchased on 1 January 1994 for £100,000. It was lived in as the taxpayer's main residence until 31 January 2024, at which time work began to convert the property into three flats. The work was completed in April 2024, and the flats were sold in July 2024 for £275,000 each. The conversion work cost £180,000.

At first sight, it may seem that the entire gain is covered by private residence relief as it had been the taxpayer's home throughout the period of ownership. However, there is a trap that will catch the unwary. This is because private residence relief is denied in respect of a gain in so far that it is attributable to any expenditure that is incurred after the beginning of a period of ownership that is incurred wholly or partly for the purposes of realising a gain.

Broadly, the provisions work to deny private residence relief in relation to that portion of the gain that is attributable to the expenditure incurred in order to realise a higher profit. It is therefore necessary to obtain a valuation of the house assuming the work had not been carried out and it was sold as a single dwelling. In this way, it is possible to establish the additional profit attributable to the conversion work.

In the above example, it is assumed that had the property been sold as the original family home it would have fetched £600,000. By converting it into flats, the sale proceeds increased to £825,000 (3 x £275,000). The cost attributable to the additional proceeds of £225,000 (i.e. £825,000 - £600,000) is the conversion expenditure of £180,000. This expenditure effectively generated an additional gain of £45,000 (£225,000 - £180,000). The development gain does not qualify for private residence relief.

The computation of the gain is therefore as follows:

	Total Gain £	Exempt Gain £	Non-Exempt Gain £
Proceeds	825,000	600,000	225,000
Less: cost of property	(100,000)	(100,000)	
cost of extension	(180,000)		(180,000)
GAIN	545,000	500,000	45,000

The non-exempt gain is reduced by the taxpayer's annual allowance (set at £3,000 for 2024/25) to the extent that this remains available and charged to CGT at the appropriate rate. For 2024/25, this is 18% to the extent the income and gains fall in the taxpayer's basic rate band, and at 24% to the extent that they fall in the higher or additional rate band.

As the gain is a residential property gain, it must be reported to HMRC within 60 days of completion and capital gains tax on the development gain (as reduced by the annual exempt amount if available), paid within the same time frame.

21.6.4. Case Study 4 – House Converted Into Flats, One Sold, One Lived In As A Home

A homeowner decides that her house is too big for her. She converts it into two flats, one of which she sells. She continues to live in the remaining flat.

The property was purchased in 2014 for £325,000. In 2024, the property was converted into two flats. The conversion work was completed in May 2024. One flat was sold in June 2024 for £275,000. The conversion costs were £40,000. At that date, the value of the unconverted house was £500,000 and the value of the flat retained was £350,000.

The combined value of the two flats at the date the flat was sold was £625,000. This is £125,000 more than the value of the unconverted property at that date. The conversion costs are £40,000, giving rise to a gain attributable to conversion of £85,000.

This gain is not covered by the private residence exemption. However, it must be attributed between the flats to ascertain the amount that comes into charge in respect of the sale of the first flat. This is done simply on an apportionment basis by reference to the relative values of each property on the date that the first flat was sold.

The non-exempt gain attributable to the flat sold is therefore:

£275,000/£625,000 x £85,000 = £37,400.

The remainder of the gain attributable to the first flat is covered by private residence relief.

The non-exempt gain (as reduced by any allowable losses and the annual exemption to the extent that it remains available) is charged to CGT at the appropriate rate (18% or 24% depending on whether income and gains exceed the basic rate band of £37,700 or not).

How To Slash Your Property Capital Gains Tax

22. Understanding Capital Gains Tax (CGT)

Before we look at the different ways to cut your capital gains tax saving strategies, it is important to understand what is meant by the term **capital gains tax (CGT)** and when property investors are liable to pay it.

In this section you will become familiar with CGT and how it is calculated when you decide to sell your property.

22.1. When You Are Liable To Pay CGT

A property investor is likely to incur a CGT liability in the following two situations:

a) when a property is sold at a higher price than for which it was purchased;

b) when a property, or part of a property, is transferred to a non-spouse.

> Properties and other assets can be transferred between husband and wife living together freely, without triggering a CGT liability.

Both of the above situations are illustrated in the following case studies.

CGT Liability When Selling a Property

Maria purchases a buy-to-let property in January 1998 for £100,000. She rents it out for five years and then sells it for £210,000.

This means that she has made a capital gain of £110,000, upon which she is liable to pay CGT.

CGT Liability When Transferring a Property

Maria purchases a buy-to-let property in January 1998 for £100,000. She rents it out for five years and then gifts the property to her mother.

She receives no payment from her mother for the property.

Although Maria has received no payment for the property, she is treated as having transferred the property to her mother at 'market value,' which is £210,000. Therefore, again, Maria is liable to pay CGT on the £110,000 profit.

> Property dealers/traders are not liable to pay CGT. When they sell a property, the profit is classed as a dealing profit, and therefore they are liable to pay **income tax** on the profits.

22.2. How Your CGT Bill Is Calculated

Calculating the tax liability on the sale or transfer of a property is not easy.

Given the property price increases over the past few years alone, investors are sitting on significant capital gains.

It is important to realise that a number of reliefs and strategies are available to reduce any CGT liability you may have. The most significant of these are detailed in the remainder of this guide.

However, listed in the table below are the typical reliefs/reductions that can be claimed when a property is sold/transferred.

If applicable, these can be offset against the capital gain made on the property and can be used to significantly reduce any tax liability.

Relief/Reduction	Description
Buying and Selling Costs	Typical purchase costs include: • solicitor' fees; • estate agency fees • survey costs; • cost of searches, e.g., land, mining, etc. • stamp duty land tax Typical selling costs include: • estate agency fees; • solicitor' fees;
Capital Costs	If you have incurred costs of a capital nature, then these can also be offset. A capital cost is one that has increased the price of the property. Examples of capital costs include the building of conservatories, additional bedrooms, loft conversions, garage conversions, etc.

Indexation Relief	This relief was available for qualifying for property that was sold by individuals before April 6th, 2008. The actual indexation stopped at April 1998.
Private Residence Relief	This relief is based on the period that the property was classed as your PPR.
Private Letting Relief	This relief is a relief for a property that was at one time your private residence that can reduce your capital gain by up to an additional £40,000. It was available up until 5th April 2020 in all circumstances, but for disposals after that date only where the landlord has occupied the property at the same time as the tenant.
Allowable Losses	If you have incurred capital losses, then these can be offset against any capital gain made when you dispose of your property.
Taper Relief	This relief was introduced in April 1998 and was a replacement for indexation relief. However, it can only be claimed for property sold before 6th April 2008.
Personal CGT Allowance	For the 2023-24 tax year it is £6,000. For the 2024-25 tax year it is £3,000.

23. Reporting And Tax Payment Changes From 6th April 2020

From a capital gains tax (CGT) perspective, making a gain on a property that has always been the owner's only or main residence is a 'good thing' as the gain can be enjoyed free of tax, even if the owner jumps off the property ladder following the sale.

However, when it comes to gains on residential property where full private residence relief is not available, the tax regime is increasingly punitive; not only does a higher rate of tax apply to residential property gains than other gains (with the exception of carried interest), from April 2020 the timescale for reporting such gains to HMRC and paying the associated tax is significantly reduced.

23.1. When May A Residential Property Gain Arise?

Private residence relief applies to shelter a property that has been the owner's only or main residence throughout the period of ownership. The availability of the final period exemption and lettings relief may mean even where a property has not always been the only or main residence, any gain can still be enjoyed free of CGT.

However, where a property has never been the only or main residence, or where relief is not available in full, a chargeable gain will arise. If it is not offset by allowable losses or covered by the annual exempt amount, CGT will be payable.

Gains made on the sale of investment properties (e.g. buy-to-let investments and second homes such as holiday homes) may give rise to a residential property gain on which CGT is payable.

The announced curtailment of lettings relief and the reduction in the final period exemption will bring more property sales within the CGT net from 6 April 2020 onwards, increasing the number of taxpayers who will be affected by the new rules.

23.2. Higher Tax Rates For Residential Property Gains

Not all gains are equal, and higher rates of CGT apply to residential property gains (and carried interest).

The rate at which CGT is payable depends on whether total income and gains exceed the basic rate limit (which has been £37,700 since 2021/22). Up to this limit, residential gains are taxed at 18% (compared to 10% for other gains); thereafter, the tax rate is 28% (compared to 20% for other gains).

23.3. Reporting Pre-6 April 2020 Residential Property Gains

Chargeable residential property gains arising prior to 6 April 2020 are reported with other gains arising in the tax year to HMRC on the CGT pages of the self-assessment return. This must be filed by 31 January after the end of the tax year to which it relates.

Gains arising in the 2019/20 tax year, including any chargeable residential property gains, must normally be notified to HMRC by 31 January 2021.

One CGT bill

Prior to 6 April 2020, the total CGT liability for the year, reflecting all chargeable gains and allowable losses (including any brought forward losses), and allowing for the annual exempt amount, is worked out as part of the self-assessment for the year. Any CGT for the year must be paid by 31 January after the end of the tax year. It is not necessary to deal with any chargeable residential property gains separately; everything goes into the pot.

This gives a lag of between nearly ten and nearly 22 months between realising the gains and reporting it to HMRC and paying the tax, depending on when in the tax year the gain arose.

23.4. New Rules From 6 April 2020

Where a residential property gain arises on a direct disposal of UK land or property by a UK resident on or after 6 April 2020, a new return must be completed and filed with HMRC within 30 days of the date of the disposal. For disposals from 27 October 2021 onwards this has been extended to within 60 days of the date of the disposal.

A return is only required where a gain is made; no return is needed if (for example) a second home or an investment property is sold at a loss. Likewise, a return is not required if the gain is entirely sheltered by private residence relief (including, where applicable, the final period exemption and lettings relief). Nor is a return required for disposals between spouses and civil partners on a no gain/no loss basis, disposals by a charity or of a pension scheme investment, or where the disposal in question is the grant of a lease at arm's length for no premium.

Once made, the return can be amended within a 12-month window, but only in respect of events that had arisen at the time the disposal was made.

23.5. Requirement To Make A Payment On Account

From 6 April 2020, a new CGT payment window applies in respect of UK residential property gains realised by a UK resident. Where such a gain is made on or after that date, a payment on account of the CGT due on that disposal must be paid within 30 days of the disposal, or 60 days for disposals from 27 October 2021 – matching the deadline for filing the associated return.

This is considerably earlier than for pre-April 2020 gains, in respect of which the normal CGT deadline of 31 January after the end of the tax year applies.

23.6. Calculating The Payment On Account

In working out the CGT on post-6 April 2020 residential property gains, the annual exempt amount can be taken into account, as can any allowable losses brought forward or realised prior to the disposal.

However, losses arising after the disposal cannot be taken into account, even if these are realised in the 30-day, or 60-day window for filing the return and making the payment on account.

23.7. Finalising The Position

In much the same way as payments on account for income tax purposes are taken into account in finalising the tax bill under self-assessment, payments made on account will be reflected in determining the overall liability for the tax year under the self-assessment position. The total CGT liability for the year will calculated (initially at least) through the self-assessment system reflecting all gains and losses in the year.

If the final bill is more than the payment made on account (e.g. because non-residential gains have also arisen in the tax year), the excess must be paid by 31 January after the end of the tax year. In the event that the final bill for the tax year is less (e.g. because losses have been realised after the residential property gain) a refund of the excess can be claimed once the self-assessment return has been filed.

> **Sale Of Holiday Home**
>
> Imogen completes on the sale of her holiday home on 10 April 2020, realising a gain of £75,000. She has made no other disposals at this point in the 2020/21 tax year. She is a higher rate taxpayer.
>
> In working out the payment on account, Imogen can take her annual exempt amount for 2020/21 into account. The chargeable gain is, therefore, £62,700 (i.e. £75,000 - £12,300) on which CGT of 28% (i.e. £17,556) must be paid by 10 May 2020. The associated return must be filed by the same date.
>
> In August 2020, Imogen sells some shares, realising a loss of £4,600. She makes no other disposals in 2020/21.
>
> For 2020/21, she realises net gains of £70,400 (£75,000 - £4,600), leaving her with chargeable gains of £58,100 after deducting her annual exempt amount of £12,300, on which the overall CGT liability is £16,268. However, Imogen has already made a payment on account of £17,556 and is, therefore, due a refund of £1,288.

24. Private Residence Relief (PPR)

In this section you will become familiar with the extremely powerful **private residence relief**.

This allowance on its own can wipe out tens or even hundreds of thousands of pounds off your chargeable capital gains.

24.1. What Is Private Residence Relief?

This relief is available to you if you have lived in a property that has been classed as your **main residence** for a period of time.

This relief is not available to you if you are a property dealer and purchased a property with the sole intention of making a dealing profit, i.e., you did not make it your main residence.

The technical name for a person's main residence is **principle private residence (PPR)**.

> If you have lived in a property that has been your PPR, then you are not liable to pay any capital gains tax on the price appreciation that is attributed to the period when you lived in the property.

There are two types of residence relief that are available, and both are described and illustrated in the following two sections.

24.1.1. Full Residence Relief

If the property has been classed as your PPR throughout your period of ownership, then you can claim **full residence relief**.

If you can claim full residence relief, then this means that you will have no CGT liability. This is regardless of the capital profit you have made on the property.

Every homeowner who has occupied their property since the first day of ownership up until the time of sale is entitled to use this relief.

Full Residence Relief

Alex buys his first home in May 2000 for £65,000. He lives in it from the day of purchase up until the day he sells it in June 2021. The selling price is £150,000, which means that he has made a capital profit of £85,000. He is not liable to pay any tax on this profit as he is able to claim full residence relief because the property was his main residence during his period of ownership.

24.1.2. Partial Residence Relief

You are able to claim **partial residence relief** if your property has been your main residence for a period of time but not for the whole period of ownership.

If you are claiming partial residence relief, then the amount of relief you can claim is determined by dividing the periods when the property was classed as your PPR by the total periods of ownership.

For example, if you purchased a property, let it out for 7 years and then lived in it for three years before selling it then you will be able to claim 3/10 partial residence relief. This is because you owned the property for 10 years, but it was your main residence for three of those years.

You are most likely to claim partial residence relief if

- you have a second home;

- you are a property investor who has let a property after having previously lived in it.

24.2. How Long In A Property Before It Can Be Classed As My PPR?

This is one of the most commonly asked tax questions.

The reason for the popularity of this question is because if you can prove that a property was genuinely your PPR, you can make use of some very generous tax reliefs. You will see in the following strategies exactly how you can use these reliefs to your advantage to reduce or even wipe out any tax liability.

HMRC have not given any specific guidance as to how long you need to live in a property before you can claim that it has been your principle private residence.

However, as a general rule of thumb, you should try to make it your permanent residence for at least one year, i.e., 12 months.

The longer you live in a property, the better chance you have of claiming residence relief.

HMRC are not necessarily interested in how long you lived in the property. They are *much more* interested in whether the property really was your home and whether you *really* did live in the property!

If you want to claim this relief, here are some pointers that will help you to convince the taxman that a property genuinely was your private residence.

    a) Have utility and other bills in your own name at the property address.

        Typical bills will include
          i. gas bills;
          ii. water rates;
          iii. electricity supply bills;
          iv. council tax bills;
          v. TV licence, etc.

b) Make the property address your voting address on the electoral register.

c) Be able to demonstrate that you bought furniture and furnishings for the property. Keep receipts and prove that bulky furniture was delivered to the property address.

d) Have all bank statements delivered to the property address.

By following the above guidelines, you will be in a good position to convince the taxman that a property was genuinely your home.

24.3. More Insight Into What Makes A PPR

A case heard by the Tax Tribunal (AJ Clarke v HMRC) has shed more light on what it takes to make a property your 'main residence' and thus exempt from capital gains tax (CGT).

Mr Clarke lived with his wife and children at Oaks Farm. His marriage was failing and he wanted to get his children away from his wife's influence. He bought 60 Nayland Road in July 2002 and moved in with his children. He had used a short term loan to buy it and needed to raise money to pay off the loan, so he obtained planning permission to build another property (58a) in the garden of No 60.

He put No 60 on the market in December 2002, only 5 months after buying it, and it sold in March 2003. He moved in with his mother while 58a was completed, and was able to occupy it in July 2003.

In July 2005, he had to move back to Oaks Farm, as his (now divorced) wife had attempted suicide and he felt he had to be there. Number 58a was put on the market and sold in November 2005.

HMRC argued that neither of the Nayland Road properties had ever been his main residence and were thus not exempt from CGT. They pointed out that he had not notified anyone of his changes of address, and correspondence for him continued to be sent to him at Oaks Farm, where he had an office from which he ran his business.

They also argued that the use of the short term loan to buy No 60 indicated that he bought it with the intention of selling it and developing another property in the garden – which of course is what he had in fact done.

Although HMRC grudgingly accepted that Mr Clarke had in fact resided at both of the Nayland Road properties, they said that his residence in both of them was merely a temporary measure and not intended to be the start of a new 'permanent home' – an expression that does not appear in the legislation, but one HMRC are fond of using in these disputes.

Mr Clarke could have made life much easier for himself if he had written to HMRC within two years of moving into No 60, nominating it as his main residence, and then done the same again when he moved into No 58a, but he had not done so within the two year time limit, so the question of which property was his main residence had to be decided on the facts.

Normally, a married couple can only have one main residence between them. The case report does not make it clear, but I assume that HMRC accepted that they were permanently separated at the time Mr Clarke bought No 60, so that potentially Mr Clarke could have a main residence of his own.

If Mr Clarke had come to me for advice, I would probably have said he had a good case as far as No 58a was concerned, as he had lived there for a couple of years, but that HMRC would probably win the argument on No 60, given how he had financed the purchase and how quickly he had put it on the market.

In fact, the Tribunal accepted that both 60 and 58a had been Mr Clarke's main residence while he occupied them, and so the gains on the sales were exempt from CGT.

They based their decision on the fact that they accepted Mr Clarke's evidence of what he had intended at the time he bought No 60 (to live there and to sell part of the land to repay the loan – the idea of building 58a had been suggested to him later by his business partner).

24.3.1. Practical Tip

The above case makes it clear that your intention when buying and moving into a property is the crucial factor in deciding whether it becomes your main residence, even if events subsequently lead you to change your mind.

24.4. Private Residence CGT Exemption - How To Lose It!

The capital gains tax (CGT) legislation which provides for relief on the disposal of a private residence includes a provision (in TCGA 1992, s 224(3)) which appears to deny the normal exemption for capital gains on a 'main residence' if you hoped to sell it at a profit when you bought it.

At the first reading, section 224 (3) seems to do away with almost all the CGT exemption. It says the main residence exemption:

"...shall not apply in relation to a gain if the acquisition of, or of the interest in, the dwelling-house or the part of a dwelling-house was made wholly or partly for the purpose of realising a gain from the disposal of it, and shall not apply in relation to a gain so far as attributable to any expenditure which was incurred after the beginning of the period of ownership and was incurred wholly or partly for the purpose of realising a gain from the disposal" (emphasis added).

Notice those two uses of 'or partly'- most of us hope to sell our homes at a profit one day, and adverts for home improvements like conservatories often make the point that this will increase the value of the property concerned. So are we all doomed to pay tax when we sell our homes? Fortunately, HMRC's Capital Gains manual instructs its staff to behave reasonably and not use the legislation in cases like these:

"It would be unreasonable and restrictive to apply the legislation in this way. The subsection should only be taken to apply when the primary purpose of the acquisition, or of the expenditure, was an early disposal at a profit" (CG65210).
HMRC generally use the legislation in three situations:

1. Quasi property development

It is difficult for HMRC to establish that someone who buys a run-down house, does it up, and then sells it in a short period of time is trading as a property developer if he genuinely lives in the property while he does so, and he has no other residence at the time, but they may use section 224(3) to charge CGT on the profit made.

2. Leasehold Enfranchisement

Tenants under a lease may get the opportunity to buy the freehold from their landlord. This is generally a sensible investment, but if you then sell the freehold shortly afterwards, you may find section 224(3) rears its head, as far as the gain attributable to the freehold is concerned.

3. Extensions and conversions

A house divided into flats will often sell for more than the same house undivided. If you do this (or build an extension) shortly before sale, then some of the gain may not be exempt.

4. Calculating the lost exemption

Except in the case of the 'property developer', it is not all of the gain that is taxed; it is only the part relating to the offending expenditure. This involves a valuation exercise.

For example, imagine a house converted into three flats and immediately sold. Each flat sells for £150,000, whereas the unconverted house would have sold for £350,000. The conversion work cost £50,000. The taxable gain is as follows:

Sale proceeds of three flats at £150,000 each	£450,000
Estimate of sale proceeds of unconverted house	(£350,000)
Gain attributable to conversion	£100,000
Less cost of conversion	(£50,000)
Taxable gain	£50,000

The longer the period between the expenditure and the sale, the less risk there is of section 224(3) being trotted out, especially if you can show another reason for the expenditure (an extension for a growing family, for example).

24.5. Private Residence Relief – When Relief May Be Restricted

No capital gains tax liability arises where a person sells his or her home provided that the property has been his or only or main residence throughout the period of ownership, except for all or any part of the last 9 months of ownership. If this condition is not met, principal private residence (PPR) relief generally applies to that fraction of the gain that related to the period for which the property was the taxpayer's only or main residence, including the last 9 months of ownership, divided by the length of ownership.

However, relief may be restricted where part of the property is used for the purposes of a trade, profession or vocation, or where there is a change in the part that is occupied as the individual's residence, or where the property was acquired wholly or partly for the purposes of realising a gain from its disposal.

24.5.1. Restriction 1 – Use For Purpose Of A Trade, Business Profession Or Vocation

By virtue of TCGA 1992, s 224(1), where a gain arises on all or part of a dwelling house, part of which is used exclusively for the purposes of a trade or business, or a profession or vocation, the gain must be apportioned between the part used as a main residence and the part used for the trade, business, profession or vocation. PPR is not available in respect of the portion of the gain that relates to the part of the dwelling house used exclusively for the purposes of the trade, profession or vocation.

It should be noted that the exclusion from PPR relief applies only to any part of the property which is used exclusively for the purposes of the trade, business, profession or vocation. Consequently, relief is not lost in relation to a room that is used for both business and private purposes. In their Capital Gains manual, HMRC cite the example of the kitchen in a small guest house which is used equally to provide meals for the guests and also to provide meals for the resident owner. As the kitchen is not used exclusively for the purposes of the trade, there is no restriction in the availability of PPR.

In a case where a part of the property is used exclusively for the purposes of a trade, business, profession or vocation, the gain must be apportioned between the residential and non-residential parts. The legislation does not provide how the apportionment must be made, and this must be determined by reference to the facts of the particular case.

Some guidance as to HMRC's approach to the apportionment calculation can be found in their Capital Gains manual. Their willingness to accept a simple apportionment based, for example, on the number of rooms used for each purposes, will depend on the tax at stake. HMRC note in their Capital Gains Tax manual (at CG64670) that in a mixed property, such as a pub with residential accommodation above, the business part would be expected to be of greater value than the residential value. Consequently, an apportionment based solely on the number of rooms or the floor area attributable to residential and non-residential use could produce an excessive amount of relief. HMRC advise their inspectors to seek a valuation from the Valuation Office Agency if an apportionment appears to be unduly weighted in favour of the residential accommodation. However, they also state that in small cases any reasonable apportionment will be accepted.

It should also be noted that HMRC do not accept computations based on taking the value of the residential accommodation in isolation and deducting it from the consideration to determine the proportion attracting relief, as this is likely to produce excessive relief.

Apportioning The Gain For PPR Purposes

Holly runs a small guest house, in which she also lives as her main residence. The property comprises twelve rooms, of which four are used exclusively for the purposes of her business. In July 2016, she sells the property for £900,000. She originally purchased the property in 1990 for £300,000. On sale she realises a gain of £600,000.

> On a simple apportionment by reference to the number of rooms, two-thirds (i.e. 8/12) of the gain would qualify for PPR relief, leaving one-third (£200,000) chargeable to capital gains tax. However, HMRC contend that a greater value attaches to the non-residential part and eventually it is agreed that the gain attributable to the part used for the business is £250,000. PPR is available in relation to the remaining gain of £350,000.

Relief is only restricted where part of the property is used exclusively for business purposes. Where a small business is run from a room in the home, ensuring that the room is also used for private purposes will preserve relief. For example, a room used as an office in the day could be used in the evenings for the children to do their homework. However, there must be some actual private use – simply leaving private possessions in the room will not be sufficient.

24.5.2. Restriction 2 – Change Of Use

A residence may be altered or extended over time and its use may change frequently. Provision is made (in TCGA 1992, s 224(2)) to ensure that where the use of the property changes, the amount of the gain qualifying for PPR is adjusted in a manner which is 'just and reasonable'.

The provisions are wide ranging in their application; they bite where there is a change in what is occupied as a person's residence as a result of the reconstruction or conversion of a building or for another reason, and there is a change in the part that is used for a trade, business, profession or vocation or for any other purposes. The adjustment to the relief will again depend on the facts in each case. However, the adjustment should reflect the extent to which, and the length of time over which, each part of the dwelling house has been used as its owner's only or main residence. Relief is allowed for the final 9 months of ownership for any part which at some time has been the owner's only or main residence.

It should be noted that this adjustment is only needed for periods where there is some residential use, but there are changes to the parts used for residential and non-residential purposes. If a property is used entirely as a main residence and is then used entirely for business purposes, relief is determined on a time-apportioned basis, with PPR relief being given for the period for which the property was the main residence or fell within the last 9 months of ownership.

24.5.3. Restriction 3 – Development Gains

The final restriction imposed by TCGA 1992, s 224 is in relation to development gains. The aim of PPR relief is to enable a homeowner to buy a property of a similar standard in a rising market. The relief is not intended to exempt speculative development gains from tax.

Relief is restricted (by s 224(3)) in circumstances in which a house is acquired wholly or partly for the purposes of realising a gain from disposal, or where there is subsequent expenditure on a property with a view to enhancing the property in order to make a gain. In the first case, no PPR relief is available. In the second case, no relief is given to the extent that the gain made relates to the enhancement expenditure incurred solely for the purposes of making such a gain.

It should be noted that the restriction is not imposed where a householder buys (say) a home in an up and coming area in the hope that it will increase in value. The legislation is intended to apply where a property is bought specifically to make a gain, for example where someone buys a rundown property, does it up in six months and sells it at a profit. In a situation such as this it is also necessary to consider whether the individual is trading. A person who is in business as a property developer will be trading and their profits on sale will be subject to income tax rather than the gain being charged to capital gains tax.

25. Increasing Property Value And Avoiding Tax

In this section you will become familiar with a tax relief that allows you to claim capital gains relief on the first 24 months of property ownership.

25.1. No CGT On The First 24 Months Of Ownership

More and more investors are increasingly facing a situation where they purchase a property but are unable to occupy it immediately due to a variety of legitimate reasons.

- You are having the property built, or
- You are altering or re-decorating the property, or
- You remain in your old home whilst you are selling it.

If you are unable to move into the property immediately after you have purchased it, then it is possible to claim 24 months' relief. What this means is that the first 24 months of ownership will still be exempt from any capital gains tax. This is regardless of whether you currently have another property that is your main residence.

However, in order to claim this relief, you *must* occupy the property within 24 months of the purchase. And a condition of the relief is that after moving in you stay in the property long enough for it to become your qualifying main residence.

For disposals on or after 6 April 2020, new legislation provides for relief for a period between the acquisition of land, including land on which a dwelling house stands, and the beginning of residence in a dwelling house on that site. There are a number of conditions which have to be satisfied which are:

- the time at which the dwelling-house or the part of the dwelling-house first became the individual's only or main residence ("the moving-in time") was within the first 24 months of the individual's period of ownership, and
- at no time during the period beginning with the individual's period of ownership and ending with the moving-in time was the dwelling-house or the part of the dwelling-house another person's residence, and
- during the period beginning with the individual's period of ownership and ending with the moving-in time a qualifying event occurred. Qualifying events are:
    - the completion of the construction, renovation, redecoration or alteration of the dwelling-house or the part of the dwelling-house; or
    - the disposal by the individual of, or of an interest in, any other dwelling-house or part of a dwelling-house that immediately before the disposal was the individual's only or main residence.

Where these conditions are satisfied the dwelling-house or part of a dwelling-house is treated as having been the individual's only or main residence from the beginning of the individual's period of ownership until the moving-in time.

First 24 Months of Ownership

Asif lives with his family in a two-bedroom terraced house.

In January 1998 he buys a run-down three-bedroom semi-detached property that requires a significant amount of development and modernisation. The property is purchased for £70,000.

The development and modernisation work starts in February 1998 and is completed 21 months later, in November 1999. The total cost of the project is £20,000.

Before he moves into the property with his family, Asif has the property valued at £120,000. This means that the property has appreciated by £30,000 (i.e., 120,000 − (£70,000 + £20,000)).

There will be no tax liability on the gain of £30,000. This is because for the purposes of working out the number of PPR years in the capital gains tax calculation the first year can be treated as though Asif and his family actually lived in the property.

26. Nominating Residence To Avoid CGT

In this section you will understand how people with more than one family home can limit or even avoid CGT on the sale of their second homes.

26.1. Having More Than One Family Home

If you have purchased a second home over the past years, it is extremely likely that you will face a considerable CGT liability when you decide to sell it.

A common scenario for having a second home is if you live in a city/town that is close to your place of work but also own a property where you go to spend your vacations, e.g., on the southeast coast of England.

If you are able to own multiple homes, then you may well save a considerable amount of tax by nominating your residence to HMRC.

26.2. Nominating Your Residence to HMRC

If you decide to sell a property, consider nominating it as your main residence to save on tax.

In order to make a nomination you must:

a) inform HMRC in writing which property is your main residence;
b) make the nomination within two years after acquiring the second property.

> **REMEMBER:** A property cannot be nominated as your main residence if it is let out.

The following case study demonstrates how a potential CGT liability can be wiped out by nominating a different residence.

Switching Residence to Avoid CGT

Bill lives in a two-bedroom apartment in London and works as a stockbroker in the heart of the city centre. He purchased his apartment in June 2015.

In June 2019 he also decides to buy a semi-detached three-bedroom house in Southampton that is just by the coast. He starts to spend most of his weekends there with his girlfriend. At the same time he nominates the London apartment as his main residence.

In April 2021 Bill realises that his house in Southampton has significantly increased in value and that he will face a considerable CGT liability if he decides to sell.

He takes professional advice and is told to vary his nomination so that his house in Southampton is his main residence.

He therefore notifies HMRC in writing that the house in Southampton is his 'nominated' main residence. This is done in June 2021 and means that the house is treated as his main residence from June 2019, because he is allowed to backdate his variation by two years.

Bill decides to sell the house in June 2021 for a £150,000 profit and has no CGT liability. This is because the house has been his nominated main residence from June 2019 to June 2021.

Bill decides to sell his apartment in June 2025. When he does so, 8/10 of the capital gain will be exempt.

This is determined as follows.

- Bill has owned the apartment for 10 years.

- Four years partial residence relief is due because between June 2015 and June 2019 it was his classed as his main residence.

- An additional four years' partial residence relief is due because between June 2021 and June 2025 it was again classed as his main residence.

This means that by switching and nominating his main residence, Bill has totally avoided any CGT liability on his three-bedroom house and also achieved a considerable reduction in the capital gain on his London apartment.

27. Other Ways To Reduce Your CGT Bill

In this section you will learn how you can reduce your CGT liability even further by

- using your annual CGT allowance;
- offsetting previous capital losses;
- timing the sale of your property.

27.1. Using Your Annual CGT Allowance

Each individual has a capital gains tax allowance that can be claimed in the tax year. What this means is that if you have made a capital gain on the sale of an asset, then you can offset the CGT allowance for the tax year in which the asset was sold.

When making a sale with a capital gain, it is important to understand the following two key points:

- if the entire allowance has already been claimed in the tax year, then it cannot be claimed again in the same tax year;

- if part of the allowance has already been claimed in the tax year, then only the outstanding unclaimed amount can be claimed.

The CGT allowances for the current and previous tax years are detailed in the table below.

	Tax Year	
	2023-2024	2024-2025
CGT Allowance	£6,000	£3,000

The following case study helps to explain how the allowance can be used:

> **Claiming the Entire Personal CGT Allowance**
>
> Bill sells his investment property on 10th April 2022 and has a £13,300 capital gain.
>
> The only tax allowance he is able to claim is his personal CGT allowance, which is £12,300 for 2022–2023, and to date, this has not been claimed.
>
> This means that after this allowance has been deducted from his capital gain (i.e., £13,300 – £12,300) he is liable to pay tax on the remaining gain of £1,000.

If Bill sells another qualifying asset with a capital gain in the 2022–2023 tax year, then he is not able to use his personal CGT allowance again.

This is because the entire CGT allowance for that tax year has already been used.

> **Claiming Partial Personal CGT Allowance**
>
> Samantha sells her investment property on 10th April 2022 and has a £7,000 capital gain.
>
> The only tax allowance she is able to claim is his personal CGT allowance, which is £12,300 for 2022–2023, and to date, this has not been claimed.
>
> This means that she has no CGT liability as the allowance of £12,300 is greater than her £7,000 gain. Furthermore, she still has £5,300 remaining from the allowance that can be used if she decides to sell another property or qualifying asset.

27.2. Capital Losses

If you have made losses on previous 'qualifying' assets, then you can register these losses with HMRC and offset these against any future capital gains.

Examples of 'qualifying' assets include

- property (e.g., you have a number of residential investment properties);
- shares in a company (e.g., you have shares in Lloyds Bank);
- units in a unit trust.

> If you have made any losses, inform HMRC of the losses in the tax year in which they were incurred. For example, if you made a loss in a share-trading deal in May 2019, then register this with HMRC in the 2019–2020 tax return.

If you are unable to or you forget to register your losses, you can still register these losses up to four years after the end of the tax year in which the loss occurred.

This is illustrated in the following case study.

> **Claiming Partial Personal CGT Allowance**
>
> Louise buys £20,000 of shares in Marconi at the height of the technology boom in May 2000. Unfortunately, the share price crumbles, and she ends up selling the shares 12 months later for a total value of £200.
>
> This means that she has made a loss of £19,800.
>
> She is unaware that she can register this loss with HMRC so that it can be offset against any future capital gain.
>
> Had she known, she would have registered this loss in her 2001–2002 tax return.

> After her misfortunes in the stock market, Louise decides to focus on property instead and buys an apartment in Birmingham in June 2001 for £120,000. She decides to sell it in June 2004 for £170,000. This gives her a capital gain of £50,000.
>
> She takes tax advice and is told by her advisor that she is still able to register her losses with HMRC. In fact, as long as she registers the losses with HMRC by 5 April 2006, they can be offset against any future capital gain.
>
> This means that she can reduce her taxable gain on the sale of the property by £19,800 immediately.

If you have made any losses on qualifying assets, then make sure that they are registered with HMRC!

27.3. Buying And Selling Costs

What many property investors fail to realise is that if you have incurred costs when buying and selling your property, then these can also be offset when the property is sold.

Typical buying costs will include

- solicitors fees;
- surveyor costs;
- land registry fees;
- solicitor's indemnity insurance;
- local authority searches, etc.
- stamp duty land tax

Typical selling costs will include

- solicitors fees;
- estate agency fees;
- advertising costs;
- accountancy fees, etc.

27.4. Selling At The Right Time Can Save You Tax!

The time when you decide to sell a property can have a significant bearing on how much tax you will save.

Before you sell your property, make sure you consider the following key pointer.

a) Beginning/end of tax year

If you expect to dispose of a number of capital assets in the same year, then try to sell them in different years to make use of your annual CGT allowance.

With just some simple tax planning you can phase the selling of assets to make sure that you always utilise your CGT allowance.

In particular, try to make sure you use up your annual CGT allowance before the end of the tax year. This is especially the case if you intend to sell multiple assets.

> **Timing the Sale of Your Property**
>
> John owns two buy-to-let properties, and in January 2018 he decides to sell them both so he can reinvest the money into a different area. John believes that he can achieve better returns by investing into an area of major regeneration.
>
> He puts both properties on the market, and a sale is agreed on both of them.
>
> John agrees with the vendors that for the sale of one property contracts will be exchanged in the 2017–2018 tax year so that he can use the CGT allowance of £11,300 for that year.
>
> He also agrees that for the second property, the contracts will be exchanged in the second week of April 2018, again so that he can use the CGT allowance of £11,700 for the 2018–2019 tax year.

If John had sold the properties in the same tax year, then he would only have been able to use the CGT allowance on the sale of one of the properties.

28. Advanced Strategies For Avoiding CGT

This section outlines a number of additional reliefs that are available, which can help to reduce the CGT liability further in certain scenarios.

Please Note: From April 2015 the rules applying when a non UK resident sells a UK residential property, and the rules for UK capital gains tax when he does so, have changed. See the chapter: **Essential Tax Advice for International Property Investors**.

28.1. How To Claim An Additional Three Years Of PPR

If you live in a property and then vacate it but return to live in the property again, you can claim up to three years' relief. This is known as the **three years' absence relief**.

It is not necessary for the property to have been rented out during the period that it was vacated.

However, for the three years' absence relief (sandwiched between periods of actual residence) it does matter if another property was your PPR during those three years, i.e. both properties cannot be your PPR at the same time.

Claiming Additional Three Years' Absence Relief

John buys a two-bedroom property in Manchester in 1985 for £45,000 and lives in it for 10 years.

He then rents a two-bedroom house in London in 1995. He decides to rent out the house in Manchester.

He moves back to Manchester in 1998 (after three years). For the period 1995-1998, John informs HMRC that the Manchester house was his elected main residence, since he was renting in London

When John moves back to Manchester he lives there for an additional three years and then sells the property in 2001 for £250,000.

This means that the property ownership can be summarised as follows:

- 1985 to 1995 he lived in the property
- 1995 to 1998 he rented out the property
- 1998 to 2001 he returned to live in the property again

This means that John has no CGT liability when he sells the property.

This is because for thirteen years the property was his main residence. Also, he is able to claim the three years' absence relief when the property was rented out. Therefore, John has made a £205,000 tax-free capital profit!

28.2. Claiming PPR When Working Overseas

If you lived in a property and your employer required you to work overseas, then the period that you spent working overseas can also be claimed as residential relief. This relief can be claimed if you return to the same property and make it your **main residence again**. The time that you spent working overseas is irrelevant.

However, you can only claim this relief if no other residence qualifies for relief during the absence, i.e., you had no other nominated PPR.

> **Claiming PPR When Working Overseas**
>
> Alex buys a two-bedroom house in 1990 for £130,000.
>
> He works as an IT consultant, and in 1992 he is asked to work on a three-year project in the United States. He jumps at the opportunity and decides to let his property whilst working overseas. His work permit is extended and he returns to live in the house in 1999, after seven years.
>
> For the period 1992-1999, Alex informs HMRC that the two-bedroom house was his elected main residence.
>
> In 2003 he is offered a permanent position in the United States, which he accepts, so he decides to sell his UK property. He has it valued at £300,000.
>
> Alex will have no CGT liability because:
>
> - between 1990 and 1992 he lived in the property, so there is no CGT liability;
> - between 1992 and 1999 he could still claim residence relief as he was working outside the country;
> - between 1999 and 2003 the property was again his main residence.

> Even if Alex had bought a property in the United States in 1992, since he elected for the UK property to be his PPR, he could still claim relief on the UK property under overseas employment relief. If he had not elected to make the UK property his PPR, then he could not claim relief for the years 1992-1999.

28.3. Claiming PPR When Re-locating In The UK

If you live in a property and then your employer requires you to work elsewhere in the UK, then you can claim up to four years' relief. You must return to the property and make it your main residence again.

However, you can only claim this relief if no other residence qualifies for relief during the absence, i.e., you had no other nominated PPR.

> **Claiming PPR When Re-locating in the UK**
>
> John works as an IT consultant. As part of his employment contract, he works at different customer locations throughout the country.
>
> He lives in North Wales, in a house he purchased in 1995 for £60,000. However, he is assigned to a long-term project in London in 1999.
>
> His company provides him with rented accommodation in London, so he decides to live there for the duration of the project.
>
> Because he will be vacating his house in North Wales, he decides to rent it out for an annual rental income of £5,000. He is liable to pay income tax on his rental profits.
>
> John finishes his assignment in London and returns to his house in North Wales in January 2003. For the period 1999-2003, John informs HMRC that the two-bedroom house was his elected main residence.
>
> After returning to North Wales he lives in his house for a year but then decides to move back to London on a more permanent basis.
>
> His house is valued at £160,000 in February 2004. John will have no CGT liability because
>
> - between 1995 and 1998 he lived in the property, so there is no CGT liability;
> - between 1999 and 2003 the duties of UK employment required him to live elsewhere and there was no other property that was his PPR;
> - from January 2003 to February 2004 he lived in the property, so there is no CGT liability.

28.4. CGT Implications Of Providing Property To Dependent Relatives

There is no principal private residence relief available to an owner if he doesn't live in the property but his relatives do.

However, if someone owned a property on 5 April 1988 that has been continuously occupied rent-free by a dependant relative since that date, the property is exempt from CGT when the owner disposes of it.

Dependant relative is defined as the owner's own or the owner's spouse's widowed mother or any other relative unable to look after themselves because of old age or infirmity. There is another possibly tax effective way of providing a home for a relative: by acquiring a property, putting it into trust, and allowing the relative to live in it rent-free for life. However, this is a simplification of the subject, and professional advice must be sought.

29. Inheritance Tax Considerations For Landlords

29.1. Introduction To IHT Considerations

Inheritance tax is a tax on the net chargeable estate of someone who dies. Landlords, particularly those with many properties, may well leave a high value estate when they die. As the rate of inheritance tax is 40%, the associated inheritance tax (IHT) bill may be significant.

There are however ways to potentially reduce the IHT payable on death, and even where a high IHT bill is inevitable, it is possible to make provision in advance for the payment of that bill.

This chapter takes a look at some of the IHT considerations of relevant to landlords.

29.2. Nature of IHT

Inheritance tax is often described as a voluntary tax. There is no tax to pay where the value of the estate is less than the available nil rate band, or where the estate is exempt because it is left to a spouse or civil partner, or to a charity or community amateur sports club.

There are various exemptions and relief which enable someone to make gifts free, or potentially free, of inheritance tax before they day.

However, property tends to be expensive and anyone with multiple properties is likely to have a chargeable estate in excess of the nil rate band. Even where property is left to a surviving spouse or civil partner on the first death and consequently no inheritance tax is payable on their estate, IHT will need to be considered in relation to the surviving spouse's estate.

29.2.1. Nil Rate Band

A person can leave an estate free of inheritance tax up to the level of the nil rate band. The nil rate band has been set at £325,000 since 2009/10 and it is due to remain at this level for future tax years up to and including 2027/28.

Where a person has a main residence that they leave to a direct descendant, they may also be able to benefit from the RNRB. This is discussed at 30.2.4.

29.2.2. Transferable Nil Rate Band

Each spouse and civil partner has their own nil rate band. To enable a couple to leave everything to their spouse or civil partner without losing the benefit of their own nil rate band, the nil rate band is transferable between spouses and the portion of the unused nil rate band that is not used on the death of the first spouse or civil partner to die can be utilised on the by the estate of the surviving spouse or civil partner on their death. As the amount transferred is the unused proportion of the nil rate band, rather than the absolute amount, there is an automatic adjustment for any change in the value of the nil rate band between the date of first death and the date of the second death.

The executors of the surviving spouse of civil partner must claim the unused nil rate band. This is done on form IHT217.

Transfer between spouses and civil partners are exempt from IHT.

When undertaking IHT planning, consideration should be given to how the nil rate band can best be used.

29.2.3. Case Study 1; Transferable Nil Rate Band

Arthur and Agnes have been married for many years. Agnes dies in 2017 and leaves her entire estate to Arthur. Arthur dies in 2024.

His estate is able to benefit from his own nil rate band, and also the unused portion (100%) of Agnes' nil rate band.

The nil rate band available on Arthur's death is therefore £650,000 – his own nil rate band of £325,000 and Agnes' unused nil rate band of £325,000.

29.2.4. Residence Nil Rate Band

Estates can benefit from a second nil rate band – the residence nil rate band (RNRB) – where a main residence is left to a direct descendant. While this will not shelter IHT on an investment property, it can potentially reduce a landlord's IHT bill if the main residence qualifies for the relief.

The RNRB was introduced in 2017/18. It was set at £100,000 for 2017/18, £125,000 for 2018/19, £150,000 for 2019/20 and at £175,000 for 2020/21. It has remained at £175,000 since 2020/21 and is due to remain at this level for tax years up to and including 2027/28.

Unlike the nil rate band, the RNRB is only available in full if the value of estate is less than £2 million. For estates worth at least £2 million, the RNRB is reduced by £1 for every £2 by which the value of the estate exceed £2 million. This means that for 2020/21 to 2027/28 inclusive, the RNRB is not available where the value of the estate £2.35 million more. Where an estate contains multiple properties, the value of the estate may very easily top £2.35 million, with the result that the benefit of the RNRB is lost.

As with the nil rate band, the unused proportion of the RNRB on the death of the first spouse or civil partner can be claimed by the estate of the surviving spouse or civil partner on their death. This remains the case even if the first spouse died before 6 April 2017 – the date on which the RNRB was introduced. The transferable RNRB must be claimed on IHT436.

The RNRB is also available where a person downsizes and sells or gives away their home on or after 8 July 2015 and leave other assets (such as the proceeds from the sale of their home) to a direct descendant.

The combined effect of the nil rate band and the RNRB is that a married couple or civil partners can between them leave up to £1 million free IHT, as long as a main residence worth at last £350,000 is left to direct descendants and the value of the deceased's estate on each death does not exceed £2.35 million. A direct descendant is:

- A child, grandchild or other lineal descendant.
- The spouse or civil partner of a lineal descendant including their widow, widower or surviving civil partner).

A direct descendant includes a child who is or was at any time a stepchild, a person's adopted child, a child fostered by them at any time and a child in respect of whom the person was appointed as a guardian or special guardian when the child was under 18.

Siblings, nephews, nieces and other relatives not in the above list are not direct descendants.

Where the estate comprises the main home and other properties and some or all of the RNRB is available, to prevent the RNRB from being lost, where possible the main residence should be left to a direct descendant. For a couple, the RNRB can shelter IHT of up to £140,000 (£350,000 @ 40%). From a tax perspective, a more favourable outcome is achieved by leaving the main residence to a direct descendant and, say, an investment property to niece or nephew, than vice versa.

If a particular property in the portfolio is to be left to a direct descendant, consideration could be made to making that property the main home to bring it within the scope of the RNRB.

29.2.5. Exemption For Gifts To Spouses And Civil Partners

Transfers to a spouse or civil partner who is domiciled or deemed to be domiciled in the UK are exempt from inheritance tax. The exemption applies to both lifetime and death transfers and is without limit, unless the transferor was UK domiciled and the transferee was non-UK domiciled at the time of the transfer.

This allows a married couple or civil partner to leave everything to their spouse without any inheritance tax arising on the death of the first spouse or civil partner, irrespective of the value of their estate.

However, this may not always be the best solution from a tax perspective and in certain circumstances in can be beneficial to leave assets up to the value of the available nil rate band other than to the surviving spouse or civil partner.

29.2.6. Potentially Exempt Transfers

Lifetime gifts are potentially exempt from inheritance tax and are termed 'potentially exempt transfers' (PETs). The gift will only become chargeable to IHT if the transferor does not survive for seven years from the date of the gift. However, if the transferor survives at least three years from the date of the gift, the rate of tax that is applied to the gift is reduced. The percentage of the full tax charged and the effective rate of tax for gifts in the seven years prior to death is shown below.

Years between date of gift and death	Percentage of tax charged	Rate of tax on the gift
0 to 3 years	100%	40%

3 to 4 years	80%	32%
4 to 5 years	60%	24%
5 to 6 years	40%	16%
6 to 7 years	40%	8%
7 or more years	0%	0%

However, as the nil rate band is allocated to gifts in chronological order, the rate of tax sheltered by the nil rate band may be less than 40% where it is set against a PET that would otherwise have benefitted from taper relief.

While giving away assets prior to death can be beneficial from an IHT perspective, particularly if the donor survives seven years, IHT is not the only tax that needs to be considered when making a gift.

This is explored further in section 30.6.

29.2.7. Gifts Out Of Income

A person can make regular gifts out of their income without any IHT consequences, as long as the person can afford to make the payments after they have met their living costs and the gifts are paid from their regular income. Such gifts are referred to as 'normal expenditure out of income'

For a landlord with multiple rental properties and rental income in excess of that needed to meet their day-to-day living costs, this can be a useful exemption and can be used to prevent income from accumulating and forming part of the estate a death. However, the exemption only applies to regular payments and it is prudent to set up a direct debit or standing order to make the payments. For example, surplus income could be used to pay a child's rent or a grandchild's school fees.

This exemption can also be used where an IHT bill is inevitable to provide funds to pay that bill.

29.2.8. Annual Exemption

An annual exemption of £3,000 applies for IHT purposes which allows a person to give away gifts worth £3,000 in total each tax year without them being added to their estate. The annual exemption can be used to give gifts or £3,000 to one person or gifts totalling £3,000 to several people. Where the annual exemption is not used on year, it can be carried forward to the following year (meaning that a person can make up to £6,000 of tax-free gifts in that year).

If the unused exemption is not used in the following year, it is lost. The current year exemption must be used before any unused exemption from the previous tax year.

29.2.9. Other Exempt Gifts

A person can give as many gifts of up to £250 per person in a tax year, as long as the recipient has not benefitted from another allowance (such as a gift on marriage).

Tax-free gifts can also be made on the occasion of a marriage or a civil partnership. The exemption applies to gifts of up to £5,000 where the recipient is a child, gifts of up to £2,500 where the recipient is a grandchild or great-grandchild and £1,000 where the recipient is another person. A wedding gift can be combined with another allowance (such as the annual exemption), with the exception of the small gifts allowance.

The exemptions limit tax-free gifts that can be made from capital.

Regular gifts made out of income can be made without limit. I.

29.2.10. Business Property Relief

Business property relief (BPR) reduces the value of a qualifying business or assets when working out how much IHT has to be paid on the estate. There are two rates of BPR – 100% and 50%. The relief applies where qualifying property is passed on while the transferor is alive or as part of the Will. Relief can be claimed on property and building, unlisted shares and machinery.

BPR at 100% is available on:
- A business or interest in a business.
- Shares in an unlisted company.

BPT at 100% is available on:
- Shares controlling more than 50% of the voting rights in a listed company.
- Land, buildings or machinery owned by the deceased and used in a business in which they were a partner or which they controlled.
- Land, buildings or machinery used in the business and held in a trust that it has the right to benefit from.

To qualify for the deceased must have owned the business or the asset for at least two years before they died.

BPR is not available where the company mainly deals in securities, stocks or share, land or buildings or the holding of investments. The final restriction poses something of a problem for landlords looking to access BPR.

BPR is not available on an asset that also qualifies for agricultural property relief. Relief is also denied if the asset was not used mainly for the business for at least two years prior to the deceased's death or if the asset isn't needed for the future of the business.

29.2.11. Agricultural Relief

Agricultural property relief (APR) is available on a qualifying transfer of agricultural property, such as farmland and farm buildings (including farm cottages and farmhouses). Properties may be owned or let but must be part of a working farm. The property must have been owned for at least two years prior to the deceased's death where occupied by the owner, a company controlled by them or their spouse or civil partner and for at least seven years before the deceased's death if occupied by someone else. Properties must be occupied by someone employed in farming, a retired farm employee or the spouse or civil farmer of a deceased farm employee to qualify for the relief. The properties must also be of a size and nature to the farming activity taking place.

APR at 100% is available where:
- The person who owned the land farmed it themselves.
- The land was used by someone else on a short-term grazing licence.

- The land was let on a tenancy that commenced on or after 1 September 1995.

Relief is available at 50% in all other cases.

Transfers of agricultural land and buildings and farm equipment that do not qualify for APR may qualify for BPR.

29.2.12. Making Use Of Exemptions And Relief

Landlords looking to mitigate the IHT payable on their death should make best possible use of the nil rate bands and the available reliefs and exemptions. Strategies for doing this are discussed later in this chapter.

It is never too early to take advice, and when purchasing properties or making business decisions, the IHT implications should be taken into consideration. There is no one size fits all and the best strategy for you will depend on your personal circumstances and what you want to achieve. IHT planning should be undertaken as part of wider succession planning goals.

29.3. Benefits Of Making A Will

Inheritance tax planning will only achieve the desired result if the people you plan to inherit your estate actually do so. For example, if you want to benefit from the inter-spouse exemption and ensure that no inheritance tax is payable on your estate by leaving everything to your spouse or civil partner, this will only happen if they do, in fact, inherit everything. The only way to ensure that your estate passes in accordance with your wishes is to make a Will. In the absence of a Will, the intestacy rules will dictate who gets what. This is particularly crucial if you want to make provision for a partner to whom you are not married or in a civil partnership with as the intestacy laws make no provision for unmarried partners.

It is never too early to make a Will. Once a Will has been made, it should be kept under review and amended if your circumstances or wishes change. It is advisable that professional advice is sought.

29.3.1. Intestacy Provisions

If you die intestate (i.e. without leaving a valid Will), the intestacy laws will dictate how you estate is distributed. Under these rules only married and civil partners and some close relatives will inherit – the rules do not make any provision for unmarried partners or cohabiting partners.

29.3.2. Surviving spouse or civil partner and surviving children

Where the deceased leaves a surviving spouse or civil partner and at least one surviving child, and the estate is valued at more than £270,000, the surviving spouse or civil partner inherits:

- All personal property and belongings of the deceased.
- The first £322,000 of the estate.
- Half the remaining estate.

The remaining half of the estate is passed to the children and divided equally among them. If a child of the deceased has died before the deceased, their share passes equally to their children.

If the estate is valued at less than £322,000, the surviving spouse or civil partner inherits everything.

29.3.3. Surviving spouse or civil partner but no children

If the deceased dies intestate but has no children, grandchildren or great grandchildren, the surviving spouse or civil partner inherits:

- All personal property and belongings of the deceased.
- The whole estate.

29.3.4. No Surviving Spouse Or Civil Partner But Children

If the deceased was not married or in a civil partnership or is a widow or widower and has children, the whole estate passes to the children who inherit equally when they reach the age of 18. Biological and adopted children are treated equally.
If a child died before the deceased and they have children, their share is inherited by their children.

Grandchildren and great grandchildren can only inherit the estate of a person who has dies intestate if their parent or grandparent died before the person who died intestate. Where this the case, the grandchildren or greatgrandchildren will inherit (in equal shares) the share to which their parent or grandparent would have been entitled,

29.3.5. No Surviving Spouse, Civil Partner or Issue

If the deceased has no surviving spouse or civil partner or children, grandchildren, the entire estate passes in the following order:

1. Surviving parents.
2. Surviving full siblings
3. Surviving half siblings.
4. Surviving grandparents.
5. Uncles, aunts and their children.

29.3.6. No Living Relatives

Where a person dies intestate and has no living relatives, their entire estate will go to the Crown. An unmarried or cohabiting partner will not inherit.

29.3.7. Case Study 2 – Operation Of The Intestacy Rules

Bernard had been planning to make a Will. However, he dies suddenly on 10 April 2024 before he had got round to it. He leaves an estate valued at £3 million, including several investment properties. He has two children, Becky and Beatrice.
He had planned to leave his entire estate to his wife Beryl.

As the intestacy provisions apply, Beryl inherits his personal possessions, valued at £100,000, the first £322,000 and 50% of the remaining £2.578 million – a further £1,289 million.

The total amount inherited by Beryl is £1,711 million.

The remaining £1,289 million is shared equally between Becky and Beatrice.

The £1.711 million inherited by Beryl is covered by the inter-spouse exemption and free from inheritance tax.

The nil rate band of £325,000 is deducted from the remaining £1,289 million, leaving a chargeable estate of £864,000 on which IHT at 40% is payable. The IHT payable by the estate is £385,600.

As the value of the estate exceeds £2.35 million, the residence nil rate band is not available.

Had Bernard made a Will and left everything to Beryl as planned, no IHT would have been payable. His failure to make a Will means that not only does his property not pass in accordance with his wishes, the estate also has to pay £385,000 in IHT which would not have been payable had he made a Will.

Making a Will is essential to ensure IHT is not paid unexpectedly.

29.3.8. Post-Death Variation

Where the deceased has died leaving a Will, it may become apparent that less IHT could have been paid by the estate had the deceased made different provisions. Where this is the case, it is not too late to undertake some tax planning as it is possible to vary the Will within two years of the date of death, as long as any beneficiary who is left worse off as a result of the changes to the Will agree to the changes.

A Will can be varied:

1. To reduce the amount of IHT or capital gains tax that is payable.
2. Provide for someone who has been left out of the Will.
3. Move the deceased's assets into a trust.
4. Provide clarification where there is uncertainty in the Will.

To change the Will after death, a Variation must be made. The Variation must meet certain conditions. These are set out in the Inheritance Tax: Instrument of Variation checklist (IOV2), which is available on the Gov.uk website.

If, as a result of the Variation of the Will, more IHT is payable, this must be paid to HMRC within six months of the date of Variation.

29.3.9. Case Study 3 - Post-Death Variation

Christine dies on 1 May 2024 leaving an estate valued at £2 million. She leaves her share in their home, worth £500,000, to her husband. Her remaining estate is left equally between her husband, Charlie and her children Craig and Caroline. Her husband received £1 million (house plus one third of remaining £1.5 million) and the children receive £500,000 each.

The £1 million left to her husband is covered by the inter-spouse exemption. The £1 million left to the children is not exempt. After deducting the nil rate band of £325,000, her net estate is £675,000 on which IHT of £270,000 is payable.

To prevent the estate having to pay IHT of £270,000, the children and Charlie vary the Will within two years of Christine's death so £325,000 is passed equally to the children and the remainder to Charlie. This saves IHT of £270,000.

29.4. Jointly Owned Property

Under English property law, there are two ways in which property can be owned jointly – as joint tenants and as tenants in common. The way in which jointly held property is owned will dictate what happens when one of the co-owners dies. Regardless of whether the property is owned as joint tenants or as tenants in common, the deceased's share forms part of their estate.

When undertaking IHT planning landlords should consider how joint properties are held and whether the current ownership structure would give the desired outcome should one of the co-owners die.

29.4.1. Joint Tenants

Where a property is owned as joint tenants, the owners together own all of the property equally – together they own the whole rather than each owning a specified share. All joint owners will have their names on the deeds, but if one of the co-owners dies, ownership passes to the other joint owners. The deeds are changed to the names of the surviving co-owner or owners once a death certificate has been provided to Land Registry.

Spouses and civil partners generally opt to own property together as joint tenants to ensure that it passes to the surviving spouse or civil partner on death; particularly where the property in question is the main residence in order to provide security to the surviving spouse or partner that they will not need to leave their home following their partner's death.

Under the survivorship rules, where a property is owned as joint tenants it automatically passes to the surviving joint owners on death. Thus, where a property is owned by spouses or civil partners as joint tenants, it will automatically pass to the surviving spouse or civil partner on death and benefit from the spouse exemption, and ownership as joint tenants may be preferred for this reason.

Landlords who are not spouses or civil partners may wish to consider holding investment properties as tenants in common to prevent their share in the property passing to the other joint owners.

Where the property is let, the income tax implications should also be borne in mind.

29.4.2. Tenants in Common

Property can also be owned jointly is as tenants in common. Where this route is taken, each joint owner owns a specified share of the property. That share is theirs to do with what they choose. On death, their share is distributed in accordance with their Will – it does not pass automatically to the other joint owners.

Prior to the introduction of the transferable nil rate band, property was often owned as tenants in common to prevent the nil rate band being wasted on the death of the first spouse or civil partner by passing the deceased's share to the children rather than the surviving spouse. Property purchased jointly prior to October 2007 by spouses and civil partners may be owned as tenants in common for this reason.

Ownership as tenants in common is popular where the joint owners are not in a relationship, for example, if a group of friends buy a property together. However, it can also be beneficial for married couples and civil partners to own property as tenants in common, rather than as joint tenants, as it allows for an element of flexibility when tax planning which is not available where a property is owned as joint tenants.

Where property is owned as tenants in common and the ownership shares are not specified, the owners are deemed to own the property in equal shares. Therefore, where spouse or civil partners own a property jointly as tenants in common, unless otherwise agreed, each will own a 50% share.

On death, where property is owned as tenants in common, the deceased's share will pass in accordance with their Will (or under intestacy laws where there is no Will). If it is left to the surviving spouse, it will benefit from the spouse exemption. Where it is left to a beneficiary other than a spouse or civil partner, the nil rate band will be available (as will the residence nil rate band where the main residence is left to children or other direct descendants). This can be an attractive option to shelter the property against care costs, or where property prices are expected to increase faster than any rise in the nil rate band, which is likely in the current market.

29.5. Making Use Of The Nil Rate Bands

As noted at 30-2-2, individuals have an IHT nil rate band available to them of £325,000. In addition, where the value of their estate is less than £2.35 million, they will benefit from an additional nil rate band (the RNRB: see 30.2.4) if they leave their main residence to a direct descendant or descendants, such as children or grandchildren. Any unused portion of the nil rate band or RNRB can use used by the estate of the surviving spouse or civil partner on their death.

The availability of the nil rate bands provide a number of tax planning opportunities for landlords.

29.5.1. Leave Property Valued Up To £325,000 Other Than To A Spouse / Civil Partner

Anything left to a spouse or civil partner is covered by the inter-spouse exemption and free from IHT. While a surviving spouse or civil partner's estate can benefit from their deceased partner's nil rate band if it is not used, it can be beneficial to utilise on the first death to protect against future increase in value, potentially reducing the IHT on the surviving spouse's death.

29.5.2. Case Study 4 – Utilise The Nil Rate Band

Darren has a number of investment properties which he lets plus his main residence which he owns jointly on with his wife Delia.

Darren makes a Will leaving one of the investment properties which he owns in sole name to his daughter Diane. When Darren dies in June 2024, the property is worth £300,000 and covered by his nil rate band.

By leaving the property to Diane, any increase in value between his death and Delia's death is sheltered from IHT. However, if the property is not her main residence, Diane will have to pay CGT on any increase in value if she sells the property. At current rates, CGT on residential gains (at 18% or 24%) is lower than IHT (at 40%).

29.5.3. Don't Waste The RNRB

When the estate comprises several properties and the RNRB (see 30.2.2) is available, it makes sense where possible if a property is to be left to a direct descendant for this to be the deceased's main residence. If the main residence is left to someone who is not a direct descendant, for example, an unmarried partner, the RNRB is not available. Similarly, the RNRB is not available in respect of an investment property, even if this is left to a direct descendent, such as a child.

This should be taken into consideration.

29.6. Make Lifetime Gifts

As noted at 30.2.6, gifts that are made at least seven years before death can be made free of IHT. Gifts made during a person's lifetime are known as 'potentially exempt transfers' (PETs) and only become chargeable if the donor dies within seven years of making the gift. However, even if the donor fails to survive seven years from the date of the gift, the rate of tax reduces if the donor survives for at least three years.

Consequently, it can be beneficial to give away property in the hope that you will live long enough for it to fall out of your estate or for the IHT payable on the gift to be reduced.

Where a PET remains in charge, the nil rate band is set against lifetime chargeable gifts, earliest first, before the death estate, meaning where taper relief would otherwise apply, the tax saved by the nil rate band is less than 40%.

While giving away property early may seem like a worthwhile gamble from an IHT perspective, the capital gains tax implications of making the gift also need to be considered. Further, there are anti-avoidance provisions to prevent you continuing to benefit from the gift once you have given it away.

29.6.1. Gifts And CGT

While giving away property during your lifetime may potentially save IHT, the gift may trigger a capital gains tax (CGT) liability depending on whether the recipient is connected to you and whether any capital gains tax exemptions apply. Death does not count as a disposal for capital gains tax purposes, and assets left on death benefit from a tax-free uplift for capital gains tax purposes. However, there may be IHT to pay.

Giving property to a spouse is covered by the IHT inter-spouse exemption and is therefore free of IHT and is not discussed here.

However, if a lifetime gift is made to, for example, a child, the consideration for the gift is deemed to be the market value at the date of the gift. This may mean that the donor ends up with a hefty capital gains tax bill if they give an investment property which does not benefit from the main residence exemption. The donor will have no sale proceeds from the gift from which to pay the capital gains tax (which on residential property must be paid within 60 days).

29.6.2. Case Study 5 – CGT Gift Trap

Edward is a landlord with several properties in his portfolio. In a bid to reduce the IHT on his estate, he makes a lifetime gift of one investment property to his daughter Ellie. At the date of the gift, the property is valued at £500,000. It cost £200,000.
For IHT, the gift is a PET.

For CGT purposes, although Edward does not receive any consideration, the chargeable gain is computed by reference to the current market value of £500,000, resulting in a gain of £300,000. If Edward is a higher rate taxpayer who has already used his annual exempt amount, he will need to pay CGT of £72,000 (£300,000 @ 24%) within 60 days of the date of the gift.

29.6.3. Potential Double Charge

A PET is only fully exempt from IHT if the donor survives seven years from the date of the gift. If he does not live a further seven years and the gift is not sheltered by the nil rate band or inter-spouse exemption and is made to a connected person, there may be a liability to both CGT and IHT.

29.6.4. Case Study 6 – IHT and CGT Trap

Frank gives an investment property to his daughter Fiona on which he pays CGT of £56,000. At the time of the gift, it is a PET for IHT purposes.

Frank dies unexpectedly two years later. Consequently, the PET comes into charge and as he survived less than three years from the date of the gift, there is no reduction in tax. If it is not sheltered by the nil rate band, IHT will be payable at 40%. Consequently, the gift triggered a CGT liability and did not achieve its desired aim of saving IHT.

29.6.5. Beware The Gifts With Reservation Rules

Anti-avoidance rules, the Gifts With Reservation (GWR) rules, exist to prevent people giving away assets to take them outside their estate for IHT purposes, while continuing to benefit from them. They frequently bite where a person gives away their home during their lifetime, but continue to live in it.

Professional advice should be sought prior to making gifts to ensure that the gift will not be caught by these rules.

29.6.6. Pre-Owned Assets Rules

The pre-owned asset rules are another set of anti-avoidance rules which may apply. The rules impose an income tax charge where the former owner continues to benefit from the property (or from a property which he has provided the funds to purchase). The charge is an annual income tax charge based on the rental value of the property.

Care should be taken to ensure gifts do not fall foul of the anti-avoidance rules. It is advisable that professional advice is sought.

29.7. Is BPR Available?

Business property relief (see 30.2.10) is a very valuable IHT relief which can provide full relief from IHT. However, it is not available in respect of investment businesses or assets. This is a problem for landlord because the letting of property is seen as an investment activity rather than as a business.

Accessing BPR is difficult for landlords but not impossible, and where investment properties are held by a company and rented out alongside another activity that qualifies for BPR, and the property rental is ancillary to the main trade, the company's shares may qualify for BPR if the other qualifying conditions are met.

To qualify, the main activities of the company must be qualifying activities – a claim for BPR will not be allowed if the rental activity is the main activity.

Again, it is advisable that professional advice is sought.

29.8. Consider A Trust

Trusts often form a key part of IHT planning and landlords can consider using trusts to mitigate their potential IHT liability. There are different type of trusts and the tax rules depend on the type of trusts.

Trusts are complex and professional advice should be sought.

29.8.1. Discretionary Trust

Placing a property or properties in a discretionary trust is effective for taking it outside the donor's estate for IHT. However, it should be remembered that the donor no longer has use and control of that property; the trustees have full discretion.

Taking the property outside the donor's estate means that there is no IHT for his estate to pay on his death. However, this does not mean that IHT can completely be forgotten as IHT charges arise in connection with the trust.

1. An entry charge at lifetime rates (20%) is payable by the trustees when the property enters the trust if the value exceeds the available nil rate band.
2. A charge arises on every 10th anniversary of the trust based on the market value of the trust assets on the day before the 10th anniversary.
3. An exit charge arises when the property leaves the trust.

Professional advice should be taken to ascertain whether the use of a discretionary trust will be beneficial for you.

29.8.2. Nil Rate Band Trust

Nil rate band trusts used to be popular before the introduction of the transferable nil rate band in 2007. While not as valuable as they used to be, they can still be beneficial.

A nil rate band trust, as the name suggests, allows a person to transfer property up to the value of their nil rate band into trust. This can be advantageous when it is desirable for the trust assets to be protected.

29.9. Property Companies And Growth Shares

It is difficult for property companies to access BPR as explained at 30.7. However, the use of growth shares (also known as freezer shares) offer an opportunity to protect the future value of the company from IHT by creating shares that are held outside of the estate.

Where rental properties are held in a company, the value of those properties is likely to increase over time, increasing the value of the company's shares, which will be included in the shareholder's estate at death.

That increase in value can be protected from IHT by creating a new class of share (e.g. B shares) which have no voting rights and no dividend rights and a low nominal value. Once the shares have been created and allocated, the rights are changed such that future capital growth is attributed to the B shares. The B shares have little value until the company is wound up or A shares are transferred to the B shareholders on death of the A shareholder.

If this is a strategy that is of interest to you, it is advisable that professional advice is sought.

29.10. Providing For The IHT Bill

It will not always be possible prevent a sizeable IHT bill from arising. Even if everything is left to a spouse/civil partner, the issue of IHT will arise on their death.

However, steps can be taken to provide funds for the beneficiaries to be able to meet the IHT bill without having to sell the property portfolio.

29.10.1. Make Gifts From Income

If the landlord has a sizeable income which is not needed in full to meet living costs, it is possible to take advantage of the regular gifts from income exemption to make regular gifts to beneficiaries for them to invest to meet the potential future IHT bill. This will also reduce the value of the estate at death and the associated IHT bill.

29.10.2. Take Out A Whole Life Policy

The landlord could also consider taking out a whole life insurance policy to cover the potential IHT bill. As no-one knows when they will die, the policy should be a whole life policy – it would be disappointing to pay premiums for years on a policy that covered death up to age 90, for the landlord to die at 91. While whole life policies are expensive, they can pay for themselves when it comes to providing funds to meet an IHT liability. This will mean that the beneficiaries will not need to sell the properties to pay the IHT.

To prevent the policy forming part of the estate, it should be placed in trust.

30. How To Better Manage Your Landlord Taxes

A message from Amer Siddiq, founder of landlordvision.co.uk:

When I began investing in property, I naturally looked around for a software solution to help me to get better organised. I quickly realised that there was nothing suitable available and so I designed my own tool based on my personal experiences and input from other very experienced landlords.

My aim was to design an easy to use solution to overcome the five biggest property management challenges faced by landlords with growing portfolios:

- Getting better organised: cutting the time spent handling paperwork
- Staying legal: keeping track of safety certificates and legal documents
- Tenant management: accurately tracking tenant payments
- Income tax management: Knowing what is due and when
- Maintaining and growing a positive cashflow

Features include:

1) **Rent and Tenancy Management** – A flexible solution for managing rents from different tenancies including single lets, multi-lets, agency lets and LHA lets, etc. Also now has the ability to collect rents from tenants via Direct Debiting facility.

2) **Calendar Alert/Reminder System** – A total solution whereby users will be able to see all their tasks in a calendar format, including rent arrears, tenancy end dates, certificate expiry dates and insurance renewal dates, etc.

3) **Expense Management** – A comprehensive expense management system whereby users will be able to record all their property related expenses and track/report on them.

4) **Integrated Accounting Engine** – All income and expenses use best practice accounting principles, making it easy for accountants to prepare and advise landlords on their property accounts.

5) **Document Uploading** – The ability to upload and store images, documents, etc. into the software.

landlord vision

www.landlordvision.co.uk